Defying
ALL ODDS

*The Battle between Faith in God and
the Challenges of Medical Science*

GOD BLESS YOU
As you read this book

Sabina and Jermain Patterson

ISBN 978-1-0980-5220-1 (paperback)
ISBN 978-1-0980-5221-8 (digital)

Copyright © 2020 by Sabina and Jermain Patterson

All rights reserved. No part of this publication may be reproduced, distributed, or transmitted in any form or by any means, including photocopying, recording, or other electronic or mechanical methods without the prior written permission of the publisher. For permission requests, solicit the publisher via the address below.

Christian Faith Publishing, Inc.
832 Park Avenue
Meadville, PA 16335
www.christianfaithpublishing.com

Printed in the United States of America

PRAISE FOR DEFYING ALL ODDS

Sabina and Jermain's book, *Defying All Odds*, is a must-read for anyone struggling in any form of a battle that needs a divine touch by God. As you read through this book, you would discover how an unwavering faith in God triumphed over the ordeal the couple experienced and how their faith was eventually rewarded with a miracle beyond wildest imagination. This book is a thriller and full of suspense. Once you start reading, curiosity and inspiration will make you a voracious reader until you hit the last page. The finger of God runs through every page. I highly recommend it as a faith builder, and also a copy for your library and a loved one. This book will urge you to listen to your inner voice or promptings by the Holy Spirit and also emphasize that God rules in the affairs of men.

—Charles D. Boison, PhD
Author of *Spiritual Militants* and *Relationship between Family Income and Obesity*

"Weapons will form but none will prosper" is the perfect description of the Pattersons' household. In this book, we are introduced to God's grace, blessings, favor, unconditional love, and using His help to overcome the adversities of life, marriage, and ectopic pregnancy. This book has taken us on a journey, demonstrating God's unlimited power of beating the odds of fear, doubt, discouragement, pain, worry, and infertility with a heads-on approach while relying only on God.

—Theresa Deen-Kargbo

With gratitude and ceaseless appreciation to the Almighty God, the Source of our faith and strength, we dedicate this book.

To Jason, Jasmine, and Judah. May you represent and point your generation to the Almighty God with unwavering faith.

To all who find themselves in the battles of this life and yet do not waver in their faith toward God. May you find rest, safety, and joy in the Lord our God.

Jesus answered and said unto them, Verily I say unto you,
If ye have faith, and doubt not, ye shall not
only do this which is done to the fig tree,
but also if ye shall say unto this
mountain, Be thou removed,
and be thou cast into the sea; it shall be done.
—Matthew 21:21

CONTENTS

Acknowledgments 9
Preface...13
Introduction 17
Chapter 1: The Journey 21
Chapter 2: Manifesting the Gift of Creativity.....................33
Chapter 3: The Unusual Encounter: "You Are My Wife"...50
Chapter 4: Breaking News 78
Chapter 5: God Is Up to Something!................................101
Chapter 6: The Challenges of Ectopic Pregnancy............116
Chapter 7: Weapons of Our Faith......................................140

ACKNOWLEDGMENTS

There are many notable people who played significant roles in making our journey and publishing of this book a reality. First and foremost, we want to thank God for making our paths cross with all those who have been a blessing to us.

We thank Johns Hopkins Hospital for being the only hospital to take us in for a long-term admission when all the others rejected us. We were shown an immense amount of care, kindness, love, and warmth during our one-month stay, from the very beginning, all the way till the day baby Judah was discharged. God bless all the doctors and healthcare workers who played a critical role in the survival of both Judah and Sabina by God's divine power.

NOVA Pregnancy Center was one of the only places during the early stages of the pregnancy that would allow us to receive any type of prenatal care. A big thank you to all the medical personnel who treated us with so much respect and empathy.

A special thanks to Commander Charles Boison and his family who have been with us from the beginning. You all have sacrificed so much during this journey, and we would like you to know that every contribution you have made to ensure the success of this story is so greatly appreciated. Again, thank you so much!

Thank you, Bishop Kibby and the Action Chapel family, for your prayers, love, and support. It was a tumultuous journey, but having you all to back us up spiritually was an immense help. We are beyond grateful for the days and nights you have spent on your knees fighting on our behalf.

Thank you to Bishop Abraham Akesseh, who has been present before the conception of Judah, all the way until now. You have helped us get through some very egregious, life-or-death situations that plagued us during the course of this pregnancy. Without your prayers and prophecies, there's no doubt the outcome wouldn't have been as amazing as it is now.

Thank you to Pastor Sebastian and Yessenia Gonzalez for their prayers and overall support while we were in the hospital. Your friendship and love truly mean a lot to us.

A big, big thank you to my brother Napoleon and his family, who has stood with us way before Judah was born. You have always been kind to us. You were even prepared to take in the kids in case we might not have pulled through. We genuinely do not know if this would have all been possible had you guys not stepped into our life those many years ago. May God bless you, mightily. You deserve it.

We thank Father Stephen Imbarrato and Mr. Larry for helping us find a medical facility even just to do something as simple as to hear Judah's heartbeat when no other facility would take us in. You've stood with us in prayer, and we greatly appreciate all of your contributions.

We sincerely express our gratitude to Melissa Hill, our literary agent; John Prickett, publication specialist; and the entire CFP Team, who transformed our manuscript to such an awesome book.

Last but most certainly not the least, our family. If it were not for you all we would not be here. In every circumstance, both good and not so good, you have stood with us. The courage and bravery you exhibited, even when it seemed that all hope was lost, was and still is inspiring and motivational. The countless hours of hardcore prayers you spent for our sake have sustained us, and we want to thank you sincerely. We love you.

PREFACE

When God put creation into motion, He made a reservation for humanity to understand the sources and some aspects of His creation. These are documented in the Bible, according to the book of Genesis. God rested on the seventh day after creating all that He wanted. He rested because he knew what He had made was all good. In order for God to bring re-modification to what He had incepted throughout the ages, He gave the most superior of His creation, humanity, the ability to have dominion over the rest of creation. Humanity or mankind was provided with knowledge, wisdom, conscience, and the free will to think before acting. These qualities culminated into a branch of a discipline called *science*.

Over the years, science has tried to explain the origin, functionality, purpose, efficacy, and effectiveness of the workings of God and His creation. Ironically, there have been instances where science has tried to contradict the creation and operations of God. Many believe there is a conflict. However, that is not how God designed it to be. Science was meant to complement or try to explain the cause and reasons to what might often be considered a "miracle." As noted by Professor Kelling Donald, chemistry professor at the University of Richmond, Virginia, "Some questions raised by science seem to clash with parts of Christian faith." Professor Donald challenges Christians not to disconnect their mind when using their faith.

The well-celebrated scientist/physicist Galileo put it this way, "I do not feel obliged to believe that the same God who has endowed us with senses, reason, and intellect has intended us to forgo their use." It does appeal to the mind that God introduced humanity to science in order to continue what He had begun. Of course, there were no ships, washing machines, and airplanes in the Garden of Eden, but God supplied all the materials and raw products needed for the manufacturing of these machines when He founded the heavens and the earth. Because God wanted to extend His healing hands to His created beings, He gave some individuals the desire, intellect, and astuteness to study to become doctors and what have you. If we knew everything about God, He would cease to be the Almighty. Thus, when medical science comes to its wit and end, and when called upon, God intervenes to what we call miracles. Unfortunately, the medical and intellectual science acquired by many who find themselves to be atheist or unbelievers in God have valued science more than God, and hardly believes or knows that there is a higher force who supersedes medical science. There have been instances where doctors have given up on some medical cases, and when those patients or family members consulted God in prayer, miracles were produced to turn the medical situations around for the better.

In their book, *Defying All Odds*, Sabina and Jermain Patterson came into contact with a situation in which science intercepted with their faith. Medical science explained that the issue at stake, ectopic pregnancy, had a zero chance for the survival of the fetus. The couple held onto their faith, insisting that God had spoken to them that the baby would be delivered to live and fulfill his purpose. Whose report do you believe? Medical science, or what God said? This book will catapult your faith to a higher dimension for you to know that in all situations, God intervenes for those who trust Him.

INTRODUCTION

"Science is the pursuit and application of knowledge and understanding of the natural and social world following a systematic methodology based on evidence," as defined by the science council, a professional body of scientists.

"Now faith is the assurance of things hoped for, the conviction of things not seen" (Heb. 11:1).

The Pattersons' story was one hot room where science and faith in God argued each other. Science, as usual, came to the room with empirical facts to prove why it was impossible for Mrs. Patterson to get pregnant. The doctors had done several medical tests and suggested surgeries to remove her tubes. The medical indications implied that Mrs. Patterson was nearing the end of her mortal existence, so the doctors gave her the book of five wishes to sign and advised her to make the final preparations. Science carried death in test results all over her.

However, faith had the better side of Mrs. Patterson. She was an unswerving believer in the faithful God who makes a way where there's no way. There is always a slim chance in faith. Faith presents us with so tiny a hope that a few humans have dared to follow. Sometimes, faith is defined as the invisible path. But in this story, it was synonymous with patience, which is always late but worth the wait.

Faith came in the story of the Pattersons with nothing to show for but words. In the words of Mr. Patterson, God had revealed to him that his wife was pregnant, but medical tests belied his revelation. And it almost seemed ridiculous to some doctors, nurses, and even some believers that Mrs. Patterson would have the confidence in her husband's words and faith in God at a time when she was going through severe pains. And to go to the contrary to medical processes which promised her life in the face of the apparent death consuming her body. Such was the faith of the Pattersons.

Within each chapter, the battle between science and faith occurs. The book consists of chronological events in the lives of the Pattersons wherein facts of the days prove the impossibility of a rather miraculous marriage, surviving hydrosalpinx, and dying embryos all the way to surviving ectopic pregnancy. But faith in God proved otherwise.

It is written in the Book of Romans 5 that:

> Through whom we have gained access by faith into this grace in which we now stand. And we boast in the hope of the glory of God. Not only so, but we also

glory in our sufferings, because we know that suffering produces perseverance; perseverance, character; and character, hope. (Rom. 5:2–4)

As people of faith, we know the by-product or the end result of our faith in God is always a miracle. In this battle, faith rewarded the Pattersons with a miraculous baby boy who was called Judah Emmanuel Patterson. God, in some intricate windings, proved to the doctors His Grace abounds and His favor endures forever.

Most often, people want to believe what they see. They believe in facts, science, things they can touch. So much such that they forget human beings are supernatural beings, that our brains can create things and those things can manifest in real life by our faith. As human as we are, many are doubters, like the doctors who handled Mrs. Patterson's case. Perhaps, God needed those people to renew their minds about Him, so He allowed a miracle to unfold before their very eyes, the birth of Judah.

And now, God wants to renew the minds of millions and has instructed this book to be written so many could hear of yet another miracle.

CHAPTER 1

The Journey

For I know the thoughts that I think toward you, says the L<small>ORD</small>*, thoughts of peace and not of evil, to give you a future and a hope.*
—Jeremiah 29:11

STORYLINE BY SABINA PATTERSON

Thoughts floated in my head. I was a piece of wood in water as heavy thoughts crowded my mind. I was excited to return to everything I had come to like about the United States (US). It was in April 2014. I was leaving Ghana, my home country, returning to a busy life in the US. My vacation seemed long yet shortened because I could no longer take advice from my father and other relatives who were married at my age and thought I should be as well. From the cockpit of the aircraft came the smooth voice of the captain, who welcomed us on board. Shortly after his welcome, a cabin crew member took over the microphone in the aisle and instructed us to pay attention to the safety precautions on the flight. I occupied a window seat in the economy section of the aircraft. After all the prefatory activities were over for our flight to take off, I bowed my head in prayer. As in all cases, I thanked God for a successful vacation and time with my family. I prayed for His Mercies for all on board to travel back home safely.

I couldn't do without prayers. Born in Takoradi, Ghana, into a solid Christian home where both parents were staunch believers and firm in making sure all their children "carry the cross of Jesus Christ on their shoulders," prayers had become a part of me. And you will later in this book realize that as Christians, we derive our strength from prayers and we conquer all things, including what may appear impossible, by faith in God.

I was assigned a window seat aboard the aircraft, which gave me control over the opening and closing of the shutter. Soon after my prayers, I opened the shutter of my window as instructed by the cabin crew member. I looked at the clouds, and all I could do was appreciate the might of God and the beauty of creation. "We serve such a mighty God," I found my lips dallying with the lyrics:

> Mighty God, we praise Thy name!
> All the earth must bow before Thee.
> We bring thanks with loud acclaim,
> for Thy wondrous works adore Thee.
> As in ancient history,
> shalt Thou is eternal.
>
> Holy Lord, God Sabaoth!
> Lord of earth, of sea and heaven,

Leader of the heavenly host,
refuge safe and certain haven.
Honor, praise to all make known;
all is Thine and Thine alone!

While I praised God for the beauty of the earth he created, I couldn't stop my thoughts from being caught in the speed of time. The thoughts of marriage surfaced in my head again, and the voices of all the people who had advised me back home played in discordance. My face suddenly changed shape for what could be best described as a disappointment. This was because I lacked a social life in the US, and I knew I was returning to a busy scheduled work life. The only time I spend away from work is the few hours on Sundays at church. I knew it was almost difficult for me to maintain a relationship that could lead to marriage.

Soon after the aircraft stabilized amid air, the cabin crew began to wheel their trolleys in the aisle to serve us drinks. I asked for water and prayed over it. Then suddenly, a still voice whispered to me to count my blessings, the same voice that always reminded me of God's presence in my life and renewed my faith in the power of prayers. I gulped the bottle of water in one sip and closed my eyes.

Jeremiah 32:27 kept ringing in my heart as I tried to slip into sleep:

> *"Behold, I am the LORD, the God of all flesh: is there anything too hard for me?"*

As I reflected on the question, comfort, and assurance stated in Jeremiah 32:27, I could not resist the reminiscence of a miraculous story, which has always energized my faith in God. It was the story of how life regenerated into my supposed dead body in a mortuary. As Christians, we must have at least one story of God's supernatural power in our lives. A story that reminds us that the one we serve is indeed a God who causes dry bones in Ezekiel 37 to sinew together, flesh developed around them and commanded the wind to breathe into flesh, thereby bringing life to the lifeless. Such stories always seem unbelievable, but yes, they happen by faith in God and prayers. Prayers, they say, move the hand of God. As a Christian, if you have not yet witnessed or experienced a single miraculous story, please let me share mine with you.

At age twelve, one afternoon after school, while walking with my friends on the streets of *Effiakuma* in Ghana to our various houses, the clouds above us gathered and frowned to herald a downpour. We quickened our steps with the hope of reaching home before the rains arrived. People ran in a helter-skelter fashion searching for shelter of some sort. Speeding cars honked at our rather careless usage of the road, but we seemed not to care.

Just like how the rapture will take a good number of humans by surprise in spite of the many end-time revelations, the rain took us by surprise that day. It fell in large, heavy drops and we took cover under a new story building under construction.

While under the structure, I secluded myself from my friends and stood elsewhere. Though they could still see me. I sat on a block and soon, the soothing atmosphere brought sleep into my eyes. Till now, I cannot remember when the rain ceased, or when my friends left the place that almost took my life for a moment. All I remember is that I woke up in a mortuary. Just like everything passes with time, the time came for the rain to stop and when it did, my friends also fled the place where we took refuge. I later learned that they thought I had already left as well. Later in the evening, my unusual absence from home prompted my parents to make a diligent search for me. They visited every one of my friends, and they all shared the same story of how I was with them under the uncompleted building but left shortly after the rain ceased. In today's society, technological advancement has given us more reasons to be individualistic; we hardly take our eyes off screens to check who is sitting by us. We say in our minds that "it isn't my business." We have even lost a sense of society. We are no longer a community. Such was the behavior of my schoolmates that day.

After a careful search for me, my parents heard the news of the collapse of the uncompleted building, which was a popular attraction due to how long it had been standing and waiting for completion. Anytime my mother narrated this story and gets to this part where they heard the news about the collapse of the structure, she would say her "intestines started burning" immediately, and she still can't remember how she got to the scene. With the help of other onlookers, my father started removing the broken blocks, digging with hope not to find me there. But the tears in his and my mom's eyes, I was told, was enough to register their fears of the possible outcomes. Block after block, finally, the afflicted scene hit my dad with utmost dismay. His Sabina was indecently buried under a two-story building. They gathered what remained of me into a taxi and drove me to Effie Nkwanta Government Hospital where I was pronounced dead upon arrival, then later sent to the mortuary.

My mom told me, which she eventually understood as the voice of God, that something kept telling her I wasn't dead. She said the voice became stronger in her head, but she was afraid she would be labeled a madwoman if she went to the mortuary to pick up my supposed lifeless body from the floor. Whenever my mom narrated this tragic story, the scripture that came to my mind was: "I shall not die, but live. And declare the works of the Lord" (Ps. 118:17). God has already answered so many prayers, but fear is one thing holding people back from living in abundant blessings. Fear is holding you back from taking the first step toward completing the journey. Fear didn't allow my mom to hear the still gentle voice of God. It clouded her head and blocked her eyes from hearing.

In Isaiah 43:1, God says,

> "Don't fear, for I have redeemed you; I have called you by name; you are Mine."

God commands us not to fear or worry. The phrase "fear not" is used at least eighty times in the Bible, most likely because He knows the enemy uses fear to decrease our hope and limit our victories. Some have even argued that there are 365 "fear nots" in the Bible—one for each day of the year. I've been a Christian all my life now, and I'm still in awe of God, who created the universe and cares about every detail of our lives.

> We belong to an all-powerful, all-knowing, victorious father who cares deeply about us.

When we meditate on this truth, it's hard to remain fearful about the trials we face. Focusing on Him helps shift our mindset from fear to faith. Jesus himself expressed fear to the point of sweating blood, so God understands fear is natural. But whatever you're afraid of—a health crisis, family problems, financial struggles—focus on the power of the only true God who calls you by name and commands fear to flee from your heart.

A Mother's Instincts

My mother's sensitivity and receptivity to the voice of God became assets that God used in saving my life. God realized my mother was a strong enough vessel to use as a point of contact to bring me to life again, much like He sent His son Jesus Christ to Capernaum to raise Jairus's twelve-year-old daughter from the dead back to life in Luke

8:49. It was in this same way and same God who performed the same miracle at the mortuary. He whispered life into me, Sabina, a twelve-year-old daughter of Mr. Hayford, a leader of God's Church, just like Jairus was a leader in the Synagogue, too.

My eyes flicked at the sight of the dead bodies around me, something in me emboldened me to jump at the least chance of life. I screamed for help, but I couldn't even hear my own voice. I tried to raise my left hand only to feel the pains of wounds I had sustained. I tried the right, though I felt some pains with that as well, but it wasn't the same as the left. So, I raised to a noticeable height even though barely off the floor struggling to wave. I could see and hear people conversing and going about their jobs in the room. I kept on waving till one of them, wearing a bloody white apron, saw me, and I recall his comment in our local dialect and I quote, "If you are dead, keep going and stop waving us good-bye." He said this without any feeling of sympathy while he walked toward me. I held his leg firmly such that he stumbled on the dead bodies. He screamed, "The girl is not dead! The girl is not dead!"

I was removed from the mortuary and sent to the emergency unit where the doctors examined the severe injuries I had received. It was decided that I needed surgery on the injuries, especially those in my skull and legs, and on almost every part of my body.

A Father's Faith

I would later learn that my dad's faith in God is the reason I am now walking on both legs, because the doctors had strongly suggested amputating the left one. But my father opposed vehemently, saying the God that gave me to them has vivid plans for my life. And through the revelations that he had received, I would not be an amputee. I was walking and glorifying the Lord on both legs. So I guess you can say my unbendable faith in the power of God's words and revelations is hereditary. A faith that would triumph over science in the battle against ectopic pregnancy. We will get to that in the chapters ahead and in hearing this story, you will appreciate faith in God even more.

The Recovery Process

I was in the hospital for eight good months. That was eight months without school, eight months of suffering, and eight months of miracles. My mates had graduated to the upper classes at the time I was finally discharged. I sat in a wheelchair for quite some time after my discharge. I suffered from the stigmatization that came with it. As recorded in the Bible in James 5:14, "Is anyone among you sick? Let him call for the elders of the church, and let them pray over him, anointing him with oil in the name of the Lord." Not only did I have my father who was an elder of the church constantly praying for me, but I also had the prayers of all sympathizers. I recall the morning visitations of the priest and other church members to our home. They came to pray with my family hoping God would return my legs to me totally healed. And gradually,

> *God manifested His Glory. I upgraded from sitting in a wheelchair to being aided by crutches.*

I walked using crutches for three months. There was absolute joy in seeing my full length again. There was certainty in my progress. At least, it was a sign that God was healing me. Not all healings are from taking prescribed drugs or meds, as I would like to say from my experience, although science can try and explain; but by faith and believing in God. Yes, the drugs work sometimes, but where they fail, your faith must be powerful for the hands of God to be moved in your favor. A renewed mind that believes you (the patient) will recover whatever part of your body that is dying and a faith so strong in the restoration to your personal comfort again are essentials. That is where all healing begins and that's when the right herbs or drugs will locate your body to facilitate the healing process.

Eventually, I began limping without the aid of my crutches. I saw the glory and power of God unravelling before my eyes. First, it was God bringing life to my lifeless body, then to speaking to my earthly father to not allow the doctors to amputate me, to blessing me with good enough health to be discharged after eight months of hospitalization, to taking me from the wheelchair to begin the restoration of my free movement as he had revealed to my Father, then to limping.

> *My brothers and sisters, I am a complete package of a miracle.*

To say I don't have a hip bone to support my right leg, yet I walk normally is in itself a miracle enough to prompt anyone that with God, and I repeat loudly, "All things are possible" (Matt. 19:26).

> *Faith is the will to have something almost impossible done. Will is what changes things around us.*

Merely wishing for a mountain to be moved will not cause the mountain to move, but once we attach faith, it will. The Bible makes us understand this in Matthew 17:20. Jesus told the disciples "Truly I tell you, if you have faith as small as a mustard seed, you can say to this mountain, 'Move from here to there,' and it will move. Nothing will be impossible for you."

***

Anytime I ponder over this miraculous story of my life, I get a renewed confidence because God has all of this thing called life planned! My life is a grand scheme, designed by the same hand who wrote the history of the world and my destiny. And that hand has never made a mistake. A perfect architect He is and has always been. "And we know that all things work together for good to them that love God, to those who are the called according to his purpose" (Rom. 8:28).

> *As preparation started for the landing of the aircraft, my mind was set for a miracle in my love life.*

I knew I have loved God all my life, and I knew He had a purpose for my life. That was why He didn't allow death to swallow me. That's why He didn't allow my leg to be amputated. That's why I am writing this book. And because God has a purpose for you and wants you to be strong in your faith, it is probably the reason you are reading this book now. It's not by coincidence that you are reading, it is a delicate part of the grand design of your healing, your miracle, your breakthrough. God is using these words to tell you to believe in Him. He is using my story to renew your faith, so you remain faithful to His words and the revelations to the end of your miracle.

Richmond International Airport was majestic and so was my state of mind as I walked out of the airport looking like a well-packaged miracle. I felt assured that my Heavenly Father will work out things in His own time for me.

CHAPTER 2

Manifesting the Gift of Creativity

But the Lord said to him, "Go, for he is a chosen instrument of Mine, to bear My name before the Gentiles and kings and the sons of Israel..."
—Acts 9:15

Storyline by Jermain E. Patterson

I was born in Arlington Hospital in northeastern Virginia. Back then, we lived in a small apartment in Falls Church. It was thence I derived my infant nature, which was a strict upbringing in the Lord. My parents made sure we attended church services. There was no way I was going to become anything contrary to a God-fearing young man. That is why looking back, it shocks me that my adolescent life was anything but that. My parents raised us up in the corridors of the school and church.

Life in Fairfax was very short, just when I thought my life was beginning to take shape, boxes were being stacked and placed against the wall. The next thing I knew, we were moving to a place called Dale City.

In Woodbridge, next door to Dale City, Virginia, my father owned a junkyard and sometimes, we went to work with him. It was at the scrapyard that I dug the foundations of a diligent life. It was such hard work that you couldn't go about it in any old way but one—get to work with love. That's how you work in the junkyard; you learn through sweat and hard work to appreciate what you do. To say to yourself as a man, you got to labor your strengths to be able to provide and survive. My dad was every word synonymous to hardworking.

My father is a man who believes in Jesus to the core. He wasn't always a Christian but through the in-laws got saved. Whenever my dad took us to work either after school or on weekends, we listened to him sing gospel songs as he worked all day on different car projects. So many times, he got carried away by unspeakable joy of the spirit and would scream, 'Thank you, Jesus, thank God for the spirit! I feel like preaching to somebody!' Then my siblings and I would scream "amen" in unison, then giggles would follow. We knew he was just excited about God and would see himself as a leader in a royal family of God, at least that was how we took it, a mere wish.

However, one day, he was solemn in his usual singing. He responded calmly when we greeted him. We thought bad news awaited us, but he called us all by our names and we gathered around the most hardworking man we knew. He told us God has told him to set up a place of worship at the junkyard. In other words, God has called him. In a typical childlike fashion, we hid our faces from him and giggled. My face was all wild smiles that turned into uncontrollable laughter when I took a second look at the man before us, standing there so humbled as one called of God with a pure heart. He was a pleasant sight. He knew we probably wouldn't understand his actions thereafter but suggested that we start accepting what was about to happen next; my dad would be one out of many preachers called to the ministry in the Woodbridge area.

In Scripture reading, we see the gift of creativity and how it was used to make a place of worship; a place where the children of Israel could gather together and worship God; to worship Him Who was their Creator, Savior, and Provider; to worship Him Who was their Leader and Guide as they made their way across the wilderness to the promised land. Listen to what the Bible says about Bezalel and Oholiab:

> And he hath filled him with the Spirit of God, in wisdom, understanding, knowledge and in all manner of workmanship...them hath he filled with Wisdom of heart, to work all manner of work, of the engraver, the cunning workman, and of the embroider, in blue, purple, scarlet, fine linen, of weaver, even of them that do any work, and of those that devise cunning work. (Exod. 35:31, 35)

We just read how the Lord blessed Bezalel and Oholiab. The Bible makes it plain that they were filled with the Spirit of God and that their gifts came from the Spirit of God. That's the key—it is a gift from God and by His Spirit. God didn't have to give those gifts to Bezalel and Oholiab. They didn't deserve to get those gifts. Just like my father and us were not worthy to be men of God. We saw ourselves as sinful vessels. But God gave us the gifts anyway. Why? So that God Himself would ultimately be praised, honored, glorified, and worshiped. These men were given gifts by God through His spirit. This means that praise does not go to Bezalel and Oholiab but to God who gave them their creative gifts. This further means that in using their gifts,

> *Bezalel and Oholiab glorified God by using the gifts that were given to them.*

Remember, the gift comes from God and His Spirit. This means the gift of creativity is a manifestation of the Spirit in the lives of Bezalel and Oholiab (1 Cor. 12:7). The presence of the gift in their life shows that the Spirit was living within them and was at work in them. The gift was a sign that they were Spirit-filled and Spirit-led. To use a New Testament phrase, the gift is a sign that they were born again by the Spirit of God, new creatures in Christ.

> *The gift of creativity was given to Bezalel and Oholiab "for the common good," as Paul puts it in 1 Corinthians 12:7.*

Their gift was meant to benefit the whole body. The gift was given so they could build a place where the children of Israel could answer God's call to worship Him, to offer sacrifices to Him, to offer a sin offering and thanks offerings. It was meant for the common good, so Bezalel and Oholiab were able to minister to the people of God. It was given so they could build up, encourage, and strengthen others through creative means. It was an early gift of Christ by means of His Holy Spirit.

Today, people tend to specialize in one craft whether it is painting, printing, woodworking, sculpting, making pottery, sewing, and so on. No such specialization with Bezalel and Oholiab. Theirs was a wide range of skill, ability, and knowledge. As we find in our Scripture passage:

> And he has filled him with the Spirit of God, with skill, ability and knowledge in all kinds of crafts [and then some of them are mentioned; not all of them] to make artistic designs for work in gold, silver and bronze, to cut and set stones, to work in wood and to engage in all kinds of artistic craftsmanship...He has filled them with skill to do all kinds of work as craftsmen, designers, embroiderers in blue, purple and scarlet yarn and fine linen, and weavers—all of them master craftsmen and designers. (Exod. 35:31–33, 35)

A wide range of skills and abilities and knowledge. All of them meant for the common good. All of them meant to build up the children of Israel. To end up ultimately to bring honor, praise, and glory to God.

We look ahead in Exodus and Moses inspecting everything made by Bezalel and Oholiab. What were Bezalel and Oholiab able to do with their gift of creative ability?

The tent and all its furnishings; the coverings; the ark; the table with all its articles; the pure gold lampstand; the gold altar, the anointing oil, the fragrant incense, and the curtain for the entrance to the tent; the bronze altar with its bronze grating, its poles, and all its utensils; the basin with its stand; the curtains of the courtyard; all the furnishings for the tabernacle; and the woven garments worn by the priests (Exod. 39:33–41).

Isn't that amazing? There was wood, there was cloth, there was gold, there was silver, there was bronze. There were special curtains around the Holy of Holies. There was all of this woodwork. There were all those figurines, remember, woven into the curtain. Do you remember all the seraphim and cherubim woven into the curtains hundreds and thousands of them? All of this done by Bezalel and Oholiab.

Then we go further in Scripture. God poured out the same gifts again when the temple was built by King Solomon and when it was dedicated.

The gift of creative ability was needed to make many of the same things except now they were bigger and even more elaborate.

You see, in the same way God blessed and assigned Bezalel and Oholiab, that was how God also assigned my father and us to help in getting this great task done. And God blessed us with the skill to play instruments and to win souls for Him.

He purchased a mobile trailer, which was about fifty feet long. We all came on board. We designed the interior décor with carpets and everything needed to make it a chapel. He went on to purchase other church instruments because that was what God put in his heart to do. He was told to start a church, so he needed everything that could help in making a church. He moved by faith and did what the Spirit directed him to do. My dad never did anything or went to the next stage of the building without directions from God. He waited for prompts to buy a trailer, to purchase instruments to enhance praise and worship in the sanctuary. He was himself an instrument of the Lord. "But the Lord said to him, 'Go, for he is a chosen instrument of Mine, to bear My name before the Gentiles and kings and the sons of Israel'" (Acts 9:15).

> *But the Lord said unto him, go thy way!*

The Syriac version reads, "Arise, go thy way"; make no delay, nor any excuse, there is no reason for it; nothing is to be feared from him: for he is a chosen vessel unto me; a choice and excellent one, full of the heavenly treasure of the Gospel, full of the gifts and graces of the Spirit, and so very fit and richly qualified for the use and service of Christ; and was "a vessel of desire," or a desirable one, as the Jews speak: or he was, to render the words literally, "a vessel of election"; both an instrument gathering in the election, or the elect of God, through the preaching of the Gospel; and was himself chosen of God, both to grace and glory, a vessel of mercy, and of honor prepared for glory; and was separated, predestinated, and appointed to the Gospel of God, to preach it among the Gentiles; which sense is confirmed by what follows:

> To bear my name before the Gentiles, and kings, and the children of Israel.

By "the name" of Christ was meant my father's Gospel, which is a declaration of his person, perfections, glories, and excellencies of his offices, grace, righteousness, and salvation; and to "bear" it is to preach it, to carry it about, spread abroad, and propagate it; in allusion either to the prophets of old, whose prophecies are often called a "burden," which they bore and carried to the several nations to whom they were sent; or to the Levites bearing the tabernacle of the Lord and its vessels. "Be ye clean that bear the vessels of the Lord" (Isa. 52:11). Upon which Aben Ezra has this note.

> "They are the Israelites, 'that bear the law.'"

But Saul was a chosen vessel to bear the Gospel; or to the sower of seed (Ps. 126:6), "before the Gentiles," or nations of the world; and he was an apostle and teacher of the Gentiles in faith and verity; the Gospel of the uncircumcision was particularly committed to him: and before "kings," as he did before Agrippa, king of the Jews, and before Nero, emperor of Rome; and his bonds for the Gospel, and so the Gospel through his bonds became manifest in all the palace, or court of Caesar. And before the children of Israel; the Jews, to whom Saul first preached it; but when they put it away, he turned to the Gentiles, and afterwards, before the Jews, he bore a testimony for it. Such was my father, a chosen vessel.

Talented to Play Drums

One afternoon, around 12:00 p.m., my father called all of us around the trailer. On it were displayed a set of musical instruments. He ordered my elder brother to go play the drums, so he sat in the seat and started playing the drums. My other brother joined and started playing, too. My father beckoned me to try my hands on it as well. And when I did, my display was a natural. I played as though I had been playing drums for about a couple of years. My dad then mentioned that I will be playing them from now on during the services, but we often took turns.

When I first got on the drums, I couldn't get enough of it. I kept playing for a little while.

Among the instruments were a keyboard and the guitar. My brothers and I came on board like the Jackson 5; my dad being the preacher and us handling the music aspect. The church was constituted and consecrated by the Holy Spirit.

We started a weekday and Sunday services in our community in Woodbridge. Though the attendance was a little at the beginning, it took just about two months for the church to register its first thirty to forty-five members as I recall.

My First Experience of Real-Life Deliverance

As time went on, my father invited very powerful preachers to minister the word of God. And their presence brought so many people to our church. Just like in every industry, you would also need the experience of others to help you grow in the work of the Lord.

On one occasion, he invited this one minister named Elijah in one of his programs. It was a very powerful event. It was the first time I saw people being delivered. I saw a demon manifest itself through a woman. The woman's eyes were galping out of their sockets; she screamed and spoke a strange language. She made angry gestures at the man of God.

I didn't understand anything about deliverance like I do now. That was when my church life really started. That was the first time I was introduced to a real-life deliverance.

I wanted to know how all of this worked. I wanted to know more about this God and if one day He would use me as I had seen Him use this minister. Everything I saw was a mystery.

I stayed in Dale City till I was about seven years old and then we moved to South Boston, Virginia. At the time, I didn't want to move, but my parents insisted it was the direction of God. I would soon have to leave all my friends, and as a kid, I felt that this was a big mistake. I didn't know how I was going to start another life distant from family and friends, but my parents who were already fully convinced it was the Lord's will, always said, "When God gives you a task, you don't complain or ask questions. You just obey and do it!" And so we moved.

At that tender age, God dealt well with me. He protected and hid me from a lot of things that would have caused my doom had it not been for the Lord. The environment where we found ourselves was an embodiment of drug dealers, liquor addicts, smokers, and all social vices you could think of. Almost all my friends were engaged in one or two bad habits, but for reasons beyond comprehension, God hid me from it all.

At the age of nineteen, I moved back to Dale City to live with my uncle. I knew I would have much more freedom than living with my parents. I was so relieved that I could experience the freedom I so long waited for. I could catch up on all that I missed out on growing up for all those years. Staying with my uncle gave me the chance to indulge in the street lifestyle that I was sheltered from for many years. Although my lifestyle changed a bit, I'd still make time to go to church.

My grandfather owned a church called Community Baptist Church. Despite all the bad stuff I was involved in at the time, I made time for God every Sunday morning and some weekday services as well. Everything seemed programmed—Wednesday, Bible study; Thursday night was choir rehearsal; and Sundays were devoted to God. On some Sundays, we were there all day, two services to be exact.

On Saturdays, I went to the clubs downtown Washington DC to party, but on Sundays, you'd surely find me in church singing with the congregation and sometimes with a hangover from the night before.

It is now that I have come to realize the enemy was trying to kill me. He knew God had placed something within me, so he was trying to throw me off course in my early twenties, but the good Lord had a task for me. He had chosen me to partner with Sabina to fight the battles of the Lord, just like Joshua did, a battle between faith and science.

At the age of twenty-one, I had a motorcycle. With my new motorcycle, I didn't want to go to church as often. I was always on the run. I always had somewhere to go. The club life was my new home and as soon as it opened up, I was there, especially on the weekends.

Interestingly, I always heard a tiny voice telling me, "Stop that, don't do this or that…don't go there…why are you doing this," and as hard-hearted as I had become, I ignored the voice over and over again. Sometimes, the voice grew so loud in my head that I could actually feel the sound in my ears.

In the late '90s, I was involved in a motor accident. I was on my way to deliver tickets to a dealership. I was about to clock out from work, but my boss asked me to drop some important papers off. It was a sunny day, and I had just recently purchased a brand-new 750 motorcycle fresh off the showroom floor. The sun's glare made it difficult to drive.

Saved from a Fatal Accident

As I was cruising down the road, a car was fast approaching me. The SUV and I collided, the force from the impact throwing me into the front windshield to soon flying through the air, landing about a hundred feet away from my cycle. I fell flat on my back, and onlookers thought I had died because for several minutes, I laid there quietly. I managed to move my neck a little to see the state of the motorcycle and the car.

An ambulance came to my rescue. The professionals took the helmet off my head and started asking me questions, but I just couldn't answer. The pain was very minor as I lay on the pavement. All I could quietly mutter to myself was, "God has saved me, God has saved me."

> *When I was taken to the hospital, doctors told me I was the luckiest person to come out of a motor accident.*

If it had been any other person coming from a motor accident, they would've either broken a bone, been paralyzed, or ended up dead. I came out of that crash with a fractured thumb and six stitches in my elbow.

I was later told I went through the windshield of a forerunner SUV that had collided with me head on and came out of the same windshield. They thought I was dead. That is how hard the impact was.

They said it was a miracle that I was alive because the glass didn't even penetrate my face.

One would think the accident would've slowed me down, but I had another motorcycle and that also landed me in an accident in DC. I skidded thirty-five miles an hour about a hundred feet away from my motorbike. Again, I walked away from what could have been fatal, escaping death. The miraculous thing about this is that I came out of it without even a scratch on my skin or clothes.

> *That was the second time I knew God was up to something with my life.*

I knew God had saved me from another incident that could have been disastrous for a reason that I had yet to discover.

One of my biggest weaknesses during that time was *lack of patience*. I have been operating heavy equipment for years. When I was promoted to become a supervisor years ago, my patience with my team was so thin that I ended up doing the job myself a few times. I didn't have the patience to allow them to grow into a point to maturity, nor did I have such time for carelessness to turn into carefulness.

I was critical of everything they did and needed specific results. I wasn't tolerant enough to be correcting people at every point.

One afternoon, I was on the highway and was hit with heavy traffic. I hated traffic jams. I just couldn't waste any minute of my time waiting for anything.

That day, a light bulb went off in my mind and something told me to be patient. I started laughing just as I approached my exit getting off the highway going home. God was saving and preparing me with those virtues He knew very well I lacked, but I would need in the battle ahead between faith and science. I needed patience, of course; faith in God; and to know He is the author and finisher of my life. He is the hand that wrote both my life story and that of the world. I needed to get that confirmation that God's purpose in my life was bigger than life. But I had no clue at all that I would meet a woman whose life had also been taken her through intricate windings, one who survived death, and one I'd marry and become my fighting partner in the battle of the Lord.

No weapon that is formed. No instrument of war, no sword, or spear; no instrument of persecution or torture that is made by the smith (Isa. 54:17).

Shall prosper. The sense here is that it shall not have final and ultimate prosperity. It might be permitted for a time to appear to prosper, as persecutors and oppressors have done; but there would not be final and complete success.

And every tongue. No one shall be able to injure you by words and accusations. If a controversy shall arise; if others reproach you and accuse you of imposture and deceit, you will be able ultimately to convince them of error, and, by manifestation of the truth, to condemn them. The language here is derived probably from courts of justice; and the idea is that truth and victory, in every strife of words, would be on the side of the church. To those who have watched the progress of discussions thus far on the subject of the true religion, it is needless to say that this has been triumphantly fulfilled.

> *Argument, sophism, ridicule have all been tried to overthrow the truth of the Christian religion.*

Appeals have been made to astronomy, geology, antiquities, history, and indeed to almost every department of science, and with the same want of success. Poetry has lent the charm of its numbers; the grave historian has interwoven with the thread of his narrative covert attacks and sly insinuations against the Bible; the earth has been explored to prove that "He who made the world and revealed its age to Moses was mistaken in its age;" and the records of Oriental nations, tracing their history up cycles of ages beyond the Scripture account of the creation of the world, have been appealed to, but thus far in all these contests, ultimate victory has declared in favor of the Bible. And no matter from what quarter the attack has come and no matter how much learning and talent have been evinced by the adversaries of the Bible, God has raised up some Watson, or Lardner, or Chalmers, or Buckland, or Cuvier, or Wiseman to meet these charges and to turn the scales in favor of the cause of truth. They who are desirous of examining the effects of the controversy of Christianity with science, and the results, can find them detailed with great learning and talent in Dr. Wiseman's Lectures on the connection between Science and Revealed Religion, Andover, 1837.

This is the heritage. The inheritance, which awaits those who serve God, is truth and victory. It is not gold and the triumph of battle. It is not the laurel won in fields of blood. But it is the protection of God in all times of trouble; his friendship in all periods of adversity; complete victory in all contests with error and false systems of religion; and preservation when the enemies rise up in any form and endeavor to destroy the church, and to blot out its existence and its name.

And their righteousness is of me. Or rather, "this is the righteousness, or the justification which they obtain of me; this is that which I impart to them as their justification." The idea is not that their righteousness is of him, but that this justification or vindication from him is a part of their inheritance and their portion.

CHAPTER 3

The Unusual Encounter: "You Are My Wife"

God is not a man, that he should lie, or a son of man, that he should change his mind. Has He said, and will He not do it? Or has He spoken, and will He not fulfil it...?

—Numbers 23:19

It had been a week of resuming the fast-paced life I'm used to since my arrival in the States. One night, while in my room alone, I received a call at an unusual hour of the night. It was from my pastor. When the phone on my desk rang, a feeling of annoyance came over me. Although I love my pastor, I am also a hardworking woman who enjoys her sleep when she can finally get it. I uncovered myself from the heavy blanket that enveloped me completely and managed to crane my neck to have a peep at the phone. I eventually answered the call before it dropped.

His voice was soothing and evoked in me a strange feeling when he said, "Someone is knocking at your door.

Would you open it for him?" Confused, I stammered over the phone, "But…Pastor?" I paused to align my thoughts with my words so I don't say anything to offend the man of God. Then I continued, "It is almost midnight." My pastor's voice gradually became more passionate as he asked, "Would you open the door for him, please?" I didn't know what to think again. "Behold, I stand at the door and knock. If anyone hears my voice and opens the door, I will come in and eat with him, and he with me." As if it was a deliberate attempt to get me to open the door, my pastor quoted Revelations 3:20 to silence me and my anxiety. I slipped into casual wear and headed for my main door. Pausing intermittently to reconsider the call, it dawned on me to further examine the number and the caller's voice. Did it sound like my pastor's? Could it be someone forcing my pastor to talk at gunpoint? My head was filled with disturbing thoughts and my heart full of fear, but I allowed the part of the scripture in Revelation that he had quoted to be my guide and strength. Just before I could place my hand on the handle of the door, a voice said so loud in my head, "Open the gates, that the righteous nation that keeps faith may enter in" (Isa. 26:2). That was all I needed to muster up some courage to face any threats or fears at midnight should the worst be at my doorstep. All the time to experience is always better than to wait in your comfort.

> *Life wouldn't be as we know it if humans didn't take risks and accept failure only to rise again. Such is what philosophers say that life is full of uncertainties.*

I grabbed the handle and opened the door. There I stood facing the darkness of night. There was no one outside knocking. But I wasn't too surprised. My pastor is always talking to us just the same way God speaks to him—in allegories. Like how the prophets of old received messages, in the same way, the ancient Egyptian philosophers and builders communicated instructions of their craft to each other to preserve their tradition in secrecy. My pastor was just a humble messenger. I closed my door and called him back to tell him I have understood the message.

"Did you go to open your door?"

"Yes, Pastor. I get it now," was my response.

"Well, it wasn't a physical knock. It was spiritual. It is your marital door. And the man knocking is a lighter-skinned man. He is not from Africa. He is from a different culture."

"Hahahaha...wow!" Yeah, I said what you might have said at this point, but I whispered it to myself, "This is crazy." What he added to it that almost got me was, "This man was born on a Saturday." At this point, I almost wanted to scream. This was all so unbelievable.

But we exchanged pleasantries and as usual, he ended the conversation by cracking jokes. "You're getting married to a fine angel," his words were on top of slight laughter. I didn't know how to respond because I had the initial doubt.

I believe God speaks to His children through His prophets.

But such details as those spelt in my pastor's words always brought a trace of doubt in people. I was human after all.

Three long days passed by me in the same way they come and go—work, home, then back to work. Then I had a dream I would later learn was a revelation. I saw in this dream a man in a black pair of pants wearing a white shirt and a nice-looking necktie with a matching belt and a pair of shoes. This well-dressed man approached me with a ring. I quickly snapped out of my dream by opening my eyes. I sat upright on my bed and stared on a portrait of Jesus on the wall. I stretched my hand to reach for light because all that I needed was light to see the face of the man in my dreams. I became full of happy thoughts. Tiny smiles brushed my sleepy face, and something which was gradually taking the form of laughter stood in my cheeks ready to be set free via outbursts. I finally shut my eyes again, as I hoped to see the man in my dreams, but he didn't reappear. So, I prayed that the will of God be done.

The next day was among those rare Sundays that I didn't go to church but work. That Sunday was indeed not a regular day. I didn't feel so. I felt all special, not because I had seen the man I would marry in my dreams, but because God revealed something to me about my life. Something I had so much feared and prayed for. It also meant to me that I was so close to Him that He could speak or reveal things to me directly. While trying to put things together for Monday's work, I heard a voice in my head saying, *Get up and go to the Giant Food Store* (a grocery store near where

I lived that was simply called Giant). I ignored it. But the voice insisted, and it grew in pitch, repeating that I go to the Giant for three consecutive times. I stood up and took my phone and in reluctant steps, I headed for the Giant. We are never sure of what we may do or say, but as soon as we remember that living is in doing or experiencing and not in thinking or worrying, we choose life. We go, even if they are reluctant steps that we take because we know for every single step we take in life, we have arrived at somewhere or something. We are never the same; we have become something we wouldn't have ever known if we had never taken that bold step.

> *As soon as I got to Giant, I saw something, which brought the whole world down to my shoulders.*

I felt heavy at the sight of a man in a clean white shirt, black pair of pants, necktie with exact same accessories I saw in my dreams. Instantly, my legs wouldn't listen to orders from my mind. I wanted to run, but it was as though I had been glued to the spot, like a deer in the headlights. I stood there staring at the man. After several seconds, he veered, and his gaze fell on me. He smiled. I became something I am yet to find a name for, but what I remember was that I became somehow frightened as he took quick steps toward me. He finally approached me and politely requested my number. I refused. He insisted. I refused. I took timid steps backwards, beginning what would later on become a run.

> *He followed me saying almost aloud, "God said you are my wife. Please, can I have your contact?"*

He kept following me, and it frightened me the most because it was my first time seeing the physical manifestation of God's revelation. What I mean by this is that I have had dreams upon dreams—yes, most do come true—but even those dreams come true in different forms from what I had seen in my sleep. So this was the first time I was seeing a live show of what I saw in my dream.

After creating a scene for ourselves, I finally had to reward his boldness by just calling out my mobile phone number into the air. I did it in such a rush and only once. I have wondered how he managed to save it in his head. But I would later know this man is naturally gifted at memorizing information. He stopped pursuing me after he got the number. However, my steps back to work were still hasty. Well, some people call it clipping or trotting, but if you decide to choose to call it trotting or clipping, please add that I did that with a fright attached.

To say I ended the day as the same Sabina who woke up on a Sunday not feeling like attending church would be a complete falsehood. I had changed. Something was happening in my world, and I could feel it. I felt something huge coming. I had a nostalgic feeling that it was something I wanted; well, may be needed; something I had been waiting for a very long time had just begun. But the funny side of it all was that I was frightened by my emotions. I didn't know that blessings come in sizes and that some of the sizes do scare the blessed. I have come to be a staunch believer in the saying, "The first step completes the whole journey."

May came and went just like all the other months of the year had been. I had not received any call from the strange man I had seen in my dream and who had appeared in the real world and taken my number in a dramatic scene. *Perhaps God had changed His mind about our union,* I thought. And then there was still another side of me counteracting my thoughts about God changing his mind. I stood in my bedroom one evening in front of a mirror and contemplated why this stranger never texted or called. Then I realized I couldn't have possibly thought of God changing His mind about something He had revealed to His beloved children. I struggled to recollect a quotation from Numbers, which assured me of God's immutability. I picked my phone up and tapped life into the Bible app and browsed through the book of Numbers to find chapter 23, verse 19, and I read aloud to myself:

> *"God is not a man, that he should lie, or a son of man, that he should change his mind.*

Has he said, and will he not do it? Or has he spoken, and will he not fulfil it?" I became hopeful again that in God's own time, He will make everything beautiful.

June also came with the sun. Summer was newly born, and the thoughts of my miraculous encounter with this man had been burned out of my head. I went about my usual schedule from home to work and back.

I guess you have heard people say God answers when you least expect it? Well, I had, too, but I had lost count of the days and so I wasn't expecting God to answer that prayer. Waiting became patience for me, and it lost form to something in the distant memory until finally, it didn't exist in my head. Therefore, when the call came from a strange number and the caller didn't remind me of the connection but just said, "Hey, this is Jermain," I became tense and responded aggressively, eventually hanging up on him.

He called again and I refused to answer, so I blocked his number. And then he kept texting that he wanted to meet me.

Two days later, I received another text from this strange number. It read, "Hey." I replied with an annoyed tone, "Who is hey?" He texted back with, "Can I see you?" As if he had made up his mind to scare me, he was all the time texting like a scammer or automated text, and I was replying angrily, having no clue at all; it could be the man I met because I had completely forgotten about him. "Can you see me for what?" And he didn't text back. It was as if my organs temporarily stopped functioning, and I went into a brief reflection to figure out who could be the owner of the strange number that texted me.

I snapped my fingers in the immediate space of my workplace and said, "I think I know who he might be!" At the time, I thought he might've been a customer who had a product to pick up from our company or a complaint to lodge. I went straight to my colleague to check the list of customers who were expecting parcels from us in that week, before, and after. She browsed through a long list, and there was no name like Jermain. The secretary had to use her personal phone to call the number and told him, "Good day, Jermain. Are you calling our company for inquiry or something else? Can you talk to me about it?"

He said, "No, I am not calling any company," and hung up. Immediately, the call dropped on our secretary and that was it for me. I blocked his number.

I went about the rest of my day at work feeling heavy with emotion. I felt I had become susceptible to a fraud attack. Like I've always done, I kept reassuring myself through life with God's words, and that day, my assurance came from Proverbs 10:2–3: "Treasures gained dishonestly profit no one, but righteousness rescues from death. The LORD will not allow a righteous person to starve, but he intentionally ignores the desires of a wicked person." I have tried in most parts of my life to be righteous so I knew God wouldn't allow someone to rob me or cause me harm.

The clouds above our company frowned, the wind carrying some amount of humidity. A heavy rainfall was apparent. We hurried through work in an attempt to get home before the rain arrived here. We ran helter-skelter. I bumped into someone in the parking lot, and my phone fell from my hands. The screen was completely shattered. I couldn't say I was worried or bothered because in the previous month, I had made up my mind to get a new iPhone.

So, when it happened, I muttered to myself, "Yeah, it is time I go get that iPhone!"

It was a bright day in June 2014, and I walked out of the phone store with my brand-new iPhone. I sat in my car in the parking lot of the phone store trying to get enough of my new product and familiarizing myself with its features when the first call came.

"Hey."

"Who is hey?" I retorted.

"I'm sorry, ma'am. This is Jermain." I have a soft place in my heart for people who readily accept their mistakes and say sorry. The word *sorry* when said to me seems to enter my heart to relieve everything that offended me.

"Who is Jermain?" I responded inquisitively

Then he giggled and said, "I met you at the Giant grocery store."

"At the Giant?" At this moment, I was beginning to recognize him. But I wasn't too excited that he called back.

"Okay, how may I help you?"

"Can I see you?"

I breathed heavily to register my own insecurities with meeting strangers. In America, it seems as though people lose their lives as often as cocks and hens do considering how many times we hear about it on the local news...But the faint acquaintance eased me.

"At where?"

The speed with which I replied to the above question was funny. He said we should meet at TD Bank at 8:00 p.m.

The skeptical me resumed analyzing and trying to spot any uncertainties in this conversation.

"TD Bank isn't open at 8:00 p.m.," I replied rather harshly.

But he insisted that we meet at TD Bank at 8:00 p.m. I finally had to give up because I didn't have an alternative meeting ground readily in mind.

When the call dropped, the summer rather rose high on my skin through the roof of the car. I was burning and everything inside me burned along. Thoughts. Emotions. Body. Soul. Spirit. Intestines. Where I'm from, we have a saying that fear burns intestines. So, of course, I was scared.

So 8:00 p.m. was here, and I was at TD Bank with a friend of mine. I brought her along because of security reasons. Even the Bible says in Ecclesiastes 4:9–12: "Two people are better off than one, for they can help each other succeed. If one person falls, the other can reach out and help. But someone who falls alone is in real trouble." And then it goes on to read in favor of the underlying reason for our meeting—*Likewise, two people lying close together can keep each other warm. But how can one be warm alone? A person standing alone can be attacked and defeated, but two can stand back-to-back and conquer. Three are even better, for a triple-braided cord is not easily broken.* Though I was skeptical about meeting Jermain that day, I also had a feeling that this was the right time God had appointed for us to get into a relationship. But at the same time, there was a part of me that didn't want this; I didn't feel all for it. I felt as though I was meeting just a random guy even though I had fully recognized him as the man I dreamt about who had appeared in real life the next day.

We scanned the space, and I couldn't find him. I then brought out my new iPhone to dial his number.

"Hello, Mr. Jermain, where are you?"

"Come inside!"

And it was the African woman in me that reacted. I responded, "Are you an armed robber? I am not getting inside," and then snapped my fingers in the air. I hurried to my friend who was at this point laughing at my African woman reaction and my somehow funny suspicion.

"Oh! I'm so sorry. I am not in TD Bank, I am in BB&T! Come inside!"

I said, "Okay." I could deal with an open space because it was safer out there. He couldn't possibly do harm under the eyes of many.

We got to BB&T and there he stood, rooted and looking all desperate. I approached from behind him and gently tapped on his shoulder. He seemed to have been lost from the present because when I touched his shoulders, he looked surprised.

"Hey!" Showing all thirty-two teeth in a broad smile that nearly got me to smile, too. But I have always been a hard girl, so I detained my smile. I'm not sure how it is for other cultures, but African ladies tend to act all strong and tough on the first date…Though we fall for the man, we fall in steps. We make it difficult for him to get us so that when finally, he arrives in our hearts, he has worked hard enough to get there and must enjoy the fruits of his labor. After all, it is the promise of wages that sweetens hard labor, they say.

"Yeah, I am here. How may I help you?"

> *Jermain was a bold man. Maybe it was because he had received a special authority from God! He went straight to it. "God said you are my wife. And I want to marry you."*

I laughed slightly. It wasn't that I didn't believe him, I did. God had revealed it to me, too. But I just didn't want it this way. I wanted it to begin from somewhere unknown to the known. But we just skipped everything and got straight to the proposal!

"Go back and pray to God again." I sounded as if I knew God better than he did. How dare I tell someone God has appointed to go back and ask Him if I was the one He chose for him. But I am pretty sure God understood me as a lady that I would be stubborn to give in to a sudden declaration of love, let alone a marriage proposal.

"If you need a wife, I could hook you up to some work colleagues of mine who are searching for marriage and maybe some clients, too." I further tore him apart with my words. You know how it is when ladies want to test to see how badly you want them.

For the first time since I met him, every form of smiling and grinning vanished, and his face took the shape of all forms of seriousness when he replied, "No. I know who God showed me."

As far as Jermain was concerned, he was obeying a calling. He believed in what he had seen in his dream and obeyed the still silent voice speaking to him about me. While on the other side of the matter, I was being obstinate to God's message. Well, like I later came to know it, I was becoming like my mother. She has always been stubborn to believe that voice and sometimes failed to have faith in her decisions even though she had prayed about them, and it had come to her in the form of revelation. My mother would still sometimes have her fears or doubts to act. People around say I look like her, talk like her, act like her. My best friend at work, our secretary, often said I look everything like my mom when I would show her pictures.

> *Our "date" was like a fruitless tree that grew in Jermain's backyard.*

His godsent wife didn't believe she was the chosen one for him. On the other end, it was equally a bad day for me as well. I had not allowed God's revelation to work through me. My deliberate actions prevented the glory of God from manifesting. I contemplated calling him to say yes, I accept and that we could get married the next day. But how would that make me look in Jermain's eyes and in my own eyes? I didn't want to appear desperate, and I didn't want to act in any way to inform him I had had the same dream about him, too.

On the twenty-fifth day of June, my phone beeped to reveal a text message, and I ignored it as I went about my daily activities. I was working. It beeped again and even though I wanted to ignore it once more, something told me to read the message. The first message was from Jermain that read, "Hi, how are you?" I didn't reply and went on to the second message. It was also from Jermain, asking, "Please can you come to the metro?" I left his message on read.

I received a handful of messages from him that day, which really disturbed my workflow. In those messages, he disclosed the location, address, and the times of the days in which we could meet. But none of those messages expressed love. All I saw in them was a man who was just following instructions to love me and have me love him, too. That might be my reason for not responding to any of them. I not only didn't respond, but I also didn't show up at his weird locations on the said days and times.

Those many text messages usually said something like, "Let's meet there from Wednesdays to Sundays." To me, Wednesday and Thursday were the same level of irrelevance. They walked the same way past me, and I was just a busy lady who had to work and wouldn't accede to a man's instructions or his genuine intentions. If God said I was his wife indeed, just like God had revealed to me, the same God could have revealed to him how to go about it. *Because so far, he had handled this revelation of marriage poorly*, I thought, *and I was battling thoughts of letting him go.*

However, after work on Friday, I hurried to the parking lot and sat in my car wanting to go somewhere. This urge of wanting somewhere to go to after work was quite foreign in my daily schedule, which has always been from home to work and then back home for most days including Fridays like this one. I scanned through my list of relatives in the US and friends. I then made up my mind on the spur of the moment to visit Jermain at the said location where he wanted us to meet originally. I didn't call him because some parts of me didn't want him to be there, and the remaining parts of me wanted to surprise him for no reason.

> *The Virginia weather was warm, but the same couldn't be said of me.*

I was not any friendly in mind with the idea of visiting a man I was not so sure of at an unknown location.

I got to the address and to my amazement and personal comfort, my GPS said that I have arrived at a Baptist Church. I suddenly became lighter and lighter by the seconds.

I have always been like the psalmist in chapter 122, verse 1. "A song of ascents. Of David. I rejoiced with those who said to me, 'Let us go to the house of the LORD.'" The headlights of the car revealed so many people entering and lounging around the church. A sudden happiness enveloped my heart about Jermain. But at the same time, a question crossed my mind, which made me cold again. What if he is not in the church but close by? I pushed the question further in the back of my mind behind my instant happiness of seeing the church. I was not happy because the man whose love for me I was doubting invited me to a church, but I was happy that upon all the places I could have been for a Friday night, God directed and guided me into a church, and it would be so cool and in fact, a huge jump for Jermain should he be in the church and not where the question at the back of my head was leading me to believe.

A Church Service to Remember!

She was in black dress, with black pair of matching shoes accompanied by a gentle smile on her face when she approached me at the entrance of the church. I began to feel the presence of God in her. She was one of the pastors who had come to host an event at the church. But when she spoke, her voice was as firm as a solid rock, and she had in her words some power and certainty. She said and I quote, "Woman," then paused and looked into my eyes until I couldn't hold her in mine any longer. She laughed teasingly and continued her heavy words,

> "God just spoke to me, and He said your marriage is three months away from now. Your ceremony will be officiated right here in this very church."

In some form of awakening, I turned around to examine the church to make sure I have not been there before.

"I have never been here," I found my lips murmuring the words to her.

"I am just a messenger of the Lord who said your husband is inside this church." Before I could wake from my little dream and tell her to lead me to him, she had taken some three steps away from me and was already making her entry into the church. I followed her with reluctant steps.

There were so many people inside the church. Just like the psalmist instructed us to enter his gates with thanksgiving and his courts with praises, they were singing to thank God and I joined in with my tired voice, which just couldn't help itself in the house of the Lord as I rendered praises and worship unto the Highest. There is complete joy in the house of the Lord that makes me wonder what more fun Christians were searching for when they leave the house of God to go to ungodly places.

My mother used to tell us a story about the last pew when we were kids and would tell me this story anytime I would head toward it. She said one day God visited a church and was blessing the congregation from pew to pew. He never got to those on the last pew because He was called to attend an emergency in heaven. So, God left and said He will be back. And we don't know when, but we believe He would come back to continue what He has already started. So anytime I sat on the last pew in church, I would remember my mother's little story, and it would cause me to smile.

Sometime in the service, while I made a home in the last pew, Jermain was called from the first pew to come forward. That was when I first saw him, and my heart skipped a beat. People were busily praying and crying onto God, prophecies were coming every now and then, tears flowed, the atmosphere of the church was full of the Holy Spirit, and I bet that you could feel it miles away from the premises.

Jermain knelt down in front of a pastor who was prophesying to him about his marriage. I covered my face with my hands and allowed my eyes to look at Jermain through the gaps between my fingers. I was beginning to understand him and also to finally accept what God had said.

The pastor's fingers cut through the crowd to locate my eyes and beckoned me to approach the altar. I have been called to the altar several times as someone who grew up in the church, but that Friday, when the pastor signaled me, I was not sure of what I was feeling at that moment. I was hot, very hot, shaking, and unable to think and walk properly. I managed to get to the altar. I confess though that I was aided.

When I got there, the pastor asked me if I knew the man who had knelt down. I said, "Yes. I first met him at Giant."

"Do you know his name?" the pastor asked me

"He mentioned it once, but I can't remember."

"Stand up," he instructed Jermain.

"Face each other and mention your names." People were smiling. The only people who were not smiling were both of us. The woman who had first approached me at the entrance had a special smile on her face that seemed to endorse our marriage already.

We faced each other. His gaze was stronger than mine, so I looked beyond his head as we whispered our names.

> *"You guys are a married couple. You have come home to your husband, my dear Sabina,"*

said the pastor, with a cheerful tone. The congregation was happily astonished because Jermain has been with them for ten years. For ten good years, he served the church and his God with all fervency and zeal. For ten years, he had not dated anyone in the church, and the ladies were beginning to wonder why and how. So, for a stranger to come and marry him was something they found surprising, yet they couldn't be any happier for a servant of humanity and God who has found a lover.

Prophetic Declaration of Our Soon-to-Be Union

"This day will forever be remembered because it is the manifestation of a grand design by God. It is a divine plan by God that these two people should marry," the pastor declared.

But let me add to the observation of the pastor by saying that because life itself is a divine scheme by God, people should unite in the grand design of being happy and communicating happiness. That is how living should be done. You become free from worries, fear, and anxiety when you realize that every part of your life has been designed by the God who knows the beginning of time and the end of it. It is not unto us to understand how our lives may be or how days may flow into months, and months into years, but it is entirely our responsibility to live through those moments, those days planting our hopes in the designer of our lives, the Grand Architect of the universe. The same hand that wrote the story of your life is the same hand that wrote the story of the world. So why worry about changing the hours, the characters to what you think it must be the end? Why stress to choose another ending when God has written it all to favor you in the end?

The congregation clapped and sang to grace the moment, but every sound ceased when the prophet screamed into the microphone.

"You never asked God why He wanted you both together?" His eyes were fixed on Jermain as if he expected a response from him.

But just when Jermain was making attempts to answer the pastor, he spoke again to silence Jermain and everyone in the room...

> "God brought you guys together to fight a battle. You are both warriors.

Something strange will happen immediately after your marriage, something that requires people with firm faith in God to go to war over. This war will be against the devil."

After the pastor said these words, it was so silent that when someone banged their car door in the parking lot, the sound could be easily heard by all inside the church. That was the severity of the dead silence that seized the atmosphere.

But somehow, I understood why God would want us together. When the building collapsed on me and nearly killed me, a pastor who had visited me in the hospital told me that God has given me a second chance because He needs me to do something for Him. So, all the years growing up and loving God, I had always had the feeling that I was yet to live the most difficult chapters in the story of my life. But to say I anticipated it to happen through my marriage would have been completely false. However, I was armed for the future. I was ready to fight for the Lord and win the battles of the Lord like Jephthah, the renowned general from Gilead, did in the battle against the Ephraimites. Many others like Joshua who prayed fervently in the battle against the Amorite Kings for the light of day to continue beyond night that he may complete the overthrow of his enemies, have used prayers and faith in God as vital tools of action in winning battles. So, I was somehow glad and unafraid when the pastor said we will fight a battle for the Lord. Because not only was I aware of such a thing in my life, but I armed myself with all the armor of the Lord and I was battle ready if you asked me.

People have often wondered what the armor of God is and how it can be used. Well, in Ephesians 6:10–18, the armor of the Lord and how and when to use them is literally explained. It says:

> Finally, be strong in the Lord and in his mighty power. Put on the full armor of

God, so that you can take your stand against the devil's schemes. For our struggle is not against flesh and blood, but against the rulers, against the authorities, against the powers of this dark world and against the spiritual forces of evil in the heavenly realms. Therefore, put on the full armor of God, so that when the day of evil comes, you may be able to stand your ground, and after you have done everything, to stand. Stand firm then, with the belt of truth buckled around your waist, with the breastplate of righteousness in place, and with your feet fitted with the readiness that comes from the gospel of peace.

In addition to all this, take up the shield of faith, with which you can extinguish all the flaming arrows of the evil one. Take the helmet of salvation and the sword of the Spirit, which is the word of God. And pray in the Spirit on all occasions with all kinds of prayers and requests. With this in mind, be alert and always keep on praying for all the Lord's people.

So, while Joshua and Jephthah fought against flesh and blood with physical swords and horses, in this dispensation, our battles are not physical but spiritual. That is why one must put on the armor of God to have a victory when fighting and standing for the Lord.

> *When the service was over, we were the topic of the night. It was as though the whole program was organized in the church for us two.*

We were like celebrities. We encountered many friendly conversations with other congregants. The rest of our time was spent standing in small groups either narrating how we feel toward the prophecy of our marriage or saying thank you to well-wishers.

And when all was said and done, it was just the two of us at my car in the parking lot. That was when everything that had happened played back before my eyes and mind. I explained to Jermain that I had made up my mind to not honor his invitation, which is why I had not showed up on Wednesday and Thursday like he had asked. But I don't know why that Friday after work, I got that strong urge to go somewhere other than home. And I couldn't think of anywhere else to go but to meet him. I was clueless about the church event and about the fact that my heart was going to be won completely in love.

The Beginning of Our Relationship toward Marriage

Jermain said that everything including us was part of the bigger plan that God is only using to fulfill a bigger promise or fight as revealed through the prophecy. For a while, he remained quiet, and it dawned on me that he was not ready for battle.

> *"Victory belongs to those who prepare themselves adequately for battles,"*

I whispered into his ear, and his face beamed with a smile. He felt loved and empowered. We then went our respective ways.

That was how our relationship began. Since then, I would wake up each day to Jermain's call or message. We did everything together. We prayed together. We spent time together every single day after work. My honest prayer for anyone reading this book is that I hope you find somebody to love. Love actually liberates the soul, allowing it to see beyond the flesh and carnal intents. To be truly alive is to love somebody. It is worth noting that I did not say to live is to be loved. Oftentimes, people seek to be loved more than to love somebody. Love is not a fifty-fifty affair. It is you giving all your cards away, all your one hundred without expecting returns. But since nature controls the matters of love, the person you have given your all to will eventually realize and return with even more than what you put into it. That is the hope of the faithful, and the prayer of the faithful is almost always rewarded with answers from God the Father.

United in Holy Matrimony, October 3, 2015

It was Jermain who drew most of the attention to himself without even trying. I thought brides carried the day during weddings, but during ours, the groom did. That day, he was not the usual handsome, neat, and humble guy I have known all the while. He was someone who stole the day with a uniqueness in his smile. Even his haircut was magically attractive!

Familiar and unknown faces with smiles journeyed into the church as though they had a commander who ordered them about—Smile for the day, it's a good day that the Lord has made, we will rejoice in it, stay in the procession, be beautiful for the day for we are soldiers of the Lord. It was as if the invincible commander gave these orders from behind the blue calm sky above everyone.

I was in a white silk gown with a long, luxurious train fit for a queen. It was also long enough for my family to trace my whereabouts by following the excess fabric should there be any reason for them to do so. It was my wedding day, after all!

Under a beautiful sunny Saturday morning, with beautiful faces smiling everywhere, I, Sabina Hayford, took an oath to marry Jermain Patterson and him likewise.

I don't intend to go into details here about our wedding day or the nights and the days immediately after. That would probably leave me romanticizing. That being said, if you were to ask me personally, you would be treated to a three-day-nonstop story about how happy I was and still become whenever I relive the experience. But for now, we need not change the focus of this book. We need to get diving into the battle against faith. We need to tell our testimony, so that you may hold onto the least trace of faith in God in whatever storms you are going through now.

Just like the Bishop had prophesied, there was a huge storm awaiting us as married couples. That God had foreordained our marriage because He needed the two of us, His soldiers, to be united in something as sacred as marriage in order to fight that good fight.

First Timothy 6:12 says, "Fight the good fight of faith, lay hold on eternal life, to which you were also called and have confessed the good confession in the presence of many witnesses."

Oftentimes, we wonder why we need some of these institutions of old as recommended in the Bible like marriage. But Ecclesiastes 4:9–12 tells that:

> Two are better than one because they have a good return for their labor. For if either of them falls, the one will lift up his companion. But woe to the one who falls when there is not another to lift him up. Furthermore, if two lie down together, they keep warm, but how can one be warm alone? And if one can overpower him who is alone, two can resist him. A cord of three strands is not quickly torn apart. (Eccles. 4:9–12)

> *Wholeness provides the kind of strength we need to deal with all the good and bad variables of life.*

For example, someone to rejoice with as well as someone with whom we can share sorrow. Joy is multiplied and sorrow is divided when we are whole.

Even death is better faced after living a life where we have been whole. There is less regret because we have known the ultimate experience that we, as humans, were meant to experience. As the British poet, Alfred Lord Tennyson wrote, "'Tis better to have loved and lost than never to have loved at all."

In the end, all the songs of youthful love and all the movies and books with romantic themes appeal to that particular yearning that all people have to be whole. A lifetime of faithful partnership in marriage yields the precious silver of that wholeness that Hollywood dream about and portrays on the silver screens.

Jermain was mine and I became his.

CHAPTER 4

Breaking News

So do not fear, for I am with you; do not be dismayed, for I am your God. I will strengthen you and help you; I will uphold you with my righteous right hand.

—Isaiah 41:10

"You have toxic liquids in the fallopian tubes," he said without any emotion on his face. He was straight with his answer and didn't seem to care much about how I would take the news.

"The medical term for this issue is hydrosalpinx," he continued.

"Okay?" It was that okay of mine which asked for more into what had just been said. An interrogative look was beginning to appear on my face.

"The fallopian tubes extend from the uterus, one on the right and one on the left. If they become blocked or infected, infertility may result," he further explained. His words came from a place where science obviously ruled. And I listened from a place where faith internally ruled.

He ushered me to a small test lab. I could only assume this was the place where women are told they are infertile and go down in tears, as reality forces them to embrace the truthfulness of their diagnosis.

I laid down on a tiny bed in the middle of the room filled with medical computers and machines. The doctor then whispered to me, "We are going to carry on a procedure known as sonosalpingography to find out the extent of the damage the toxic fluid has caused your tubes." I just laid there praying in my head. Whatever this man was about to do was not much of a bother to me. The words of God which my husband read to me at the dawn of that day came back to me from Psalm 90:17, "Let the favor of the Lord our God be upon us, and establish the work of our hands upon us; yes, establish the work of our hands!"

I prayed silently for the Lord's favor on my tubes. "So do not fear, for I am with you; do not be dismayed, for I am your God. I will strengthen you and help you; I will uphold you with my righteous right hand" (Isa. 41:10). As I laid there waiting for the doctor to finish preparing, I tried very hard to remember any Bible verses that talked against fear, for I was a bit afraid of the events that had begun to unfold. I wanted somewhere to plant my seeds of faith that they may blossom into trust. Psalm 56: 3 "came to mind:

> *When I am afraid, I put my trust in God."*

Fear. One of the enemy's most popular weapons that he uses against us. Worry, anxiety, fear...These can overwhelm us with a thick shadow of darkness, controlling our every move and decision.

As fragile creatures, we are susceptible to fear because most transactions in life result in activities we should worry about. Things like wars, conflicts, persecution, violence, crime, natural disasters, terrorism, economic uncertainty, unemployment, divisions, disease, and death all bring worry and fear. We fear for our children's future, we fear for our families, we fear for our financial future, we fear for our safety. The list goes on...and seems like it only gets longer.

Yet reality tells us that so much of what we spend our time worrying about never even happens. Living under the weight of the "what ifs" is a hard place to dwell.

With my eyes closed, I called all the words of encouragement to memory. I remembered several Bible verses I had read, words of life and of truth. Soaking them in, over and over, praying on them silently. Until they became so familiar, they replaced the other things in my mind that I'd battled against. There's nothing magical about words and verses, but there is power through them because they're God's words.

It's not always easy, and it often comes down to choices:

- Choosing not to allow fear and anxiety to control your life.
- Choosing to guard your heart.
- Choosing to focus your mind on what is true in the midst of uncertain times.

We might still feel afraid, but we can also believe that God is with us. We may not be in control, but we can trust the One who is. We may not know the future, but we can know the God who does because it is the same Hand who wrote your destiny that wrote the history of this world.

> He who dwells in the shelter of the Most High will rest in the shadow of the Almighty. I will say of the Lord, "He is my refuge and my fortress, my God, in whom I trust."…He will cover you with his feathers, and under his wings you will find refuge; his faithfulness will be your shield and rampart. You will not fear the terror of night, nor the arrow that flies by day, nor the pestilence that stalks in the darkness, nor the plague that destroys at midday. A thousand may fall at your side, ten thousand at your right hand, but it will not come near you…For he will command his angels concerning you, to guard you in all your ways…"Because he loves me," says the Lord, "I will rescue him; I will protect him, for he acknowledges my name. He

will call upon me, and I will answer him;
I will be with him in trouble, I will deliver
him and honor him. (Ps. 91:1–16)

A surgical trolley was wheeled to my bedside. The doctor picked up a thin tube which I later learned is called the catheter and placed this in my cervical opening. Saline solution (a sterilized salt water solution) was slowly introduced via the thin tube. The saline solution, I was told, would gently distend the uterus, so that the uterine walls move slightly away from each other.

Think of the human uterus as a deflated balloon. If you introduce a small amount of water or air, the walls of the balloon would move away from each other. This is what the saline solution does during sonohysterography, the same procedure was called sonosalpingography because it focused on the fallopian tubes.

As the saline solution is being introduced into the uterine cavity, a transvaginal ultrasound wand was used to evaluate the fallopian tubes.

If you haven't had a transvaginal ultrasound or are not familiar with it, a long, slender wand known as a transducer is used for the procedure. The wand is inserted into the vagina by the doctor.

The transducer wand emits sound waves that bounce off your body's tissues. The sound waves that bounce back are echoes, and the transducer records these echoes. The ultrasound is completely painless.

On the ultrasound screen, the doctor sees a visual representation (created with the sound waves) of your reproductive organs.

Transvaginal ultrasound can be done without the saline solution. However, it is more difficult to detect some uterine abnormalities and the true uterine shape and structure without the saline solution. When the saline solution moves the uterine walls away from each other, uterine problems are easier to see.

After few minutes, he asked me to dress up and wait for him in the consulting room adjoining the hall. I called Jermain on the phone to report. He was so worried about it all. Have you sought encouragement from a broken person before? It's like seeking for life in something that is dead.

The Doctor's Report

The doctor returned to the consulting room after several minutes. He held a white sheet in his hands. I tried to read his body language before he spoke, but his expression remained blank. Doctors have been trained to handle cases with professionalism. I know that they often mourn losses and deal with matters of love like patients do. This doctor, however, did not, and was somewhat insensitive toward the whole situation. "Unfortunately...," he paused and stared at me. As though he suddenly forgot how to say things as they were, as if he had suddenly been forced to change his trajectory.

"We would have to remove your tubes through surgery."

Those words meant that I was going to be infertile. I began questioning God. Although I had twins already from a prior marriage, I wanted to give Jermain the chance to raise up a child from infancy to adulthood. He loves my children deeply and refers to/treats them as his own. However, they are only home on the weekends and go to high school, so during the weekdays, we miss that laughter and joy from having kids at home.

It never occurred to me that this would be the reason God brought Jermain and I together.

> *I had no clue that this would be the battle of the Lord, the battle of science against faith in God.*

Science had all the facts about my infertility, science seemed to have the conviction power, science had results to prove its points. Faith wouldn't be what it is if it had facts or pictures to show as proof. Faith is having a strong belief in the unseen or unknown. It is believed that the road will reveal itself once you take the first step.

Three months had passed after the wedding. I had pelvic pains, which became acute, so I went to the hospital, only to be told now that my tubes needed to be removed.

Alexandria was like a beautiful tender old woman. Her brick sidewalks, though are centuries old, were still in shape and color. The benches along her boulevards carried lovely strangers in twos. They sat and admired the atmosphere of the historic city and the Potomac River, which runs across it. People came and went as if they were searching for their lost children or as though something dear to them was missing. They had come in search for them in Old Town Alexandria, Virginia. Everyone was caught up in the bustling atmosphere with smiles, with hearts full of problems, with good news, with their own stories weighing their shoulders down. But the people of Alexandria are not the kind who carried their stories on their faces. A perfect example of this is when I met a woman in the hospital whose daughter had just died of cancer. The woman wept bitterly in the hospital. Ten minutes later, I came to the parking lane to realize the woman's car was parked next to mine. I extended my condolences, and she just nodded without looking at me. I felt this chapter of her story was too much for her. I had forgotten about my own chapter. The woman squeezed herself into her small car and brought out her makeup kits. She started applying makeup and trying hard to bury her daughter under her skin, concealing the pain of her loss with some eye shadows. She wanted to appear normal again on the outside. After some minutes of watching her transform, she finally became a front desk banker or a receptionist. Her face became a contradiction to her moment. I stepped down out of my car and walked to hers. She lowered the window to allow herself to talk to me.

"I have indeed learned a thing from you," I said admiringly. But when she tried to respond, tears poured down on her cheeks, destroying the makeup on her face. I felt bad.

Maybe it wasn't the time for compliments or sweet talk. Maybe she wanted to appear beautiful to the world without having to mirror that beauty in her speech, because she had just lost her daughter and that indeed is a heavy loss to accept, let alone contemplate.

She brought out her makeup kit again to redo what was washed away by the tears.

"Sorry," she said while staring at her reflection in a small mirror.

> "The world is full of tears already, the least anyone can do is shine, smile, and look good.

Let someone see you and be inspired and be happy they saw you. That's how living is supposed to be." I opened my mouth in utter shock. To hear such words from a bereaved mother was so much wisdom and inspiration. That there are others who still not only care about themselves only in times of loss, but for others. She was not concerned about her worries, or so it seemed, but she was about inspiring others, making others feel good in her presence.

However, when you go to Africa, you can tell someone's story from the look on their face. You can tell life has beaten the person and that the tears had left traceable prints on their minds. Or you can predict life has been good to someone from their fleshy cheeks or the smoothness of their skin. Just like Ada. Ada was a slender lady. She was my high school mate. During my last vacation, I visited Ada at the bank where she now works as a branch manager. Clearly, she was making a lot of money because I noticed that she gained weight and was looking better than when I last saw her! In Ghana, it is a common saying that a rich and happy life means becoming all fleshy and chubby. Men in Africa joke that a protruded belly on a man meant he is a big boy, with a ton of money, living his desired lifestyle.

But unlike Ada's kind, the people of Inova Alexandria Hospital are all the same, cheerful beings with straight faces. They do not seem to care about me or about what the doctors had said to me in the hospital. Everyone seemed to be pre-occupied with their own business. Their faces don't express that they are dying, or that they are battling illnesses. So, my face did not show I was suffering from one of the big medical conditions impacting women—hydrosalpinx.

I sat in my car, straightened my dress, brushed my hair, and applied a little makeup powder and lipstick. I adjusted my face and looked all cheerful for the city. Alexandria needs light, and I was ready to provide it with the light of the Lord.

There is so much darkness engulfing the entire world, and now more than ever, we need more people smiling regardless of which chapter of their story they are living now.

Soon, I was on North Howard Street and took a left turn onto Seminary Road. I drove past trees and people without knowing what I had just driven by. I went past North Ivanhoe street and went further past North Jordan street. I went past almost everything. I was speeding past my life.

I wanted everything to pass me by. I wanted the doctor's words to join the speeding wind outside my car and pass by me as well. I just wanted to forget I visited the hospital in the first place. I was not sick. I only experienced some sharp pelvic pains from time to time. And then what? This Caucasian doctor I met at the hospital; he obviously had learned his books so well that he spoke as if he was God himself.

The sky was the only thing I couldn't go past as well as the traffic lights, considering I didn't need speeding tickets. I quickly realized that whatever I was trying to escape also traveled with me. I soon found myself at the Dunkin Donuts, soft paper napkins soaked with tears, reconstructing my face while holding a ceramic cup of coffee. I sat there contemplating what the past few hours had been. The people I have met. The news about my health. The infertility. Even the doctor's hope of saving my eggs, nothing seemed to make sense. Even Jermain's calls, which kept coming to my cell phone, irritated me. I put my phone on silent.

At Dunkin' Donuts, I saw a man who was probably weary. On his shirts were printed boldly, "Prayer is the answer." Although miniscule, strength soon came to me in that simple message, which I knew all along in life. Sometimes, we know exactly the solution to our problems. Every situation we may unfortunately or fortunately find ourselves in has the answer embedded within us. But as frail as we humans are, we break down, we worship our problems and forget about what dwells in us. We forget 1 Corinthians 10:13, which says, "No testing has overtaken you that is not common to everyone. God is faithful, and he will not let you be tested beyond your strength, but with the testing he will also provide a way out so that you may be able to endure it."

Though it isn't word for word from the Bible, it has become almost a popular saying among Christians that

> *"God won't give you more than you can handle."*

The Bible quotation above was written by the apostle Paul to the Christian church in Corinth a couple of decades after Jesus's death and resurrection. Corinth was a crossroads. It was a very cosmopolitan town with lots of activity and lots of people from different places and backgrounds. The people there would have been labeled pagans in New Testament times, meaning they were neither Jews nor Christians.

The Corinthians would have worshiped a host of various gods and goddesses, and in a host of various ways. Idolatry, drunkenness, temple prostitution was essentially the norm of the day. It was these "pagans" that made up the first Christian church in Corinth, and in following Jesus, they were called to give up their former religious practices. The problem was that they were tempted by their old ways, where all these practices were still happening right under their noses. So these early Christians struggled with sexual immorality, gluttony, and many vices. They didn't think they would be able to abandon their former lifestyle, the Corinthian way of life. But those Corinthians who remained strong and had faith in the Lord realized their sins were not too much for them to overcome and repent from and made the sacrifice to do so.

I drove back home with a renewed faith in God that He would create a way around this. I was poised for a miracle. Filled with determination,

> *I reminded myself that this was the battle God needed Jermain and I to fight, and it was the reason for our union in the first place.*

THE SCIENTIFIC FACTS BEHIND FALLOPIAN TUBES BLOCKAGE OR HYDROSALPINX

The battle between our faith in God's plan and science had just begun in our life.

> *Our story was one tense room where science and faith in God constantly argued with each other.*

Science, as usual, came to the room with empirical facts to prove why it was impossible for me to get pregnant. The doctors had done several medical tests and suggested surgery to remove my tubes. The medical indications implied that I stood the chance of ending my mortal existence if I don't get the tubes removed.

However, faith had the better side of us. I was an unswerving believer in the faithful God who makes a way where there's no way. There is always a slim chance in faith. Faith presents us with so tiny a hope that a few humans have dared to follow. Sometimes, faith is defined as the invisible path. But in this story, it was synonymous with patience, which is always late but worth the wait.

We realized medical events were going to prevent me from getting pregnant to save my life, to prove that science was all that I need. And faith was also going to make the impossible happen to disprove all the predictions of science.

But before I write about the interesting events, it would only be fair that I let you understand that this book is not meant to disprove any medical or scientific facts about the subject under discussion here. Its purpose is to inspire people's confidence in God's plan for their lives. To believe that at any point in time, a miracle can happen to change how the story is going to end for them. Miracles only happen if you believe in them.

"Science is the pursuit and application of knowledge and understanding of the natural and social world following a systematic methodology based on evidence" as defined by the science council, a professional body of scientists.

"Now faith is the assurance of things hoped for, the conviction of things not seen" (Heb. 11:1).

When we set off to write this book, I started reading more on the internet about the condition the doctor diagnosed me with in order to appreciate both sides.

Hydrosalpinx is the medical term for a fallopian tube that is blocked by a liquidly, water-like substance. If they become blocked or infected, infertility may result.

> *Getting pregnant is a pretty complicated process. At the very least, a man's sperm has to come into contact with a woman's egg in order to fertilize it.*

But sometimes, that can't happen. There are several possible reasons, one of which could be a blocked fallopian tube.

In a healthy reproductive system, the fallopian tube serves as both the pathway for an ovulated egg to reach the uterus. After an egg is released from the ovary, fingerlike projections from the fallopian tube draw the egg in.

Normally, fingerlike projections called fimbriae extend from the end of the fallopian tube close to the ovary. They help draw in the ovulated egg from the ovary into the fallopian tube. With a hydrosalpinx, the fimbriae are often damaged and stuck together.

Depending on the cause for the hydrosalpinx, additional adhesions around the fallopian tube and ovary may occur. This can also interfere with ovulation and fertility.

The irritation and/or adhesions associated with this condition could possibly lead to the fluid buildup inside the affected tube leaking into the uterus, impacting embryo implantation.

When patients go straight to in vitro fertilization (IVF) treatment without surgically removing the infected fallopian tube, pregnancy and live birth rates are much lower than would be expected. This is why many fertility specialists suggest surgical removal of the tube before beginning IVF treatment. Another option is artificial blockage of the affected tube at the uterine end, so it is less likely to affect the uterine environment.

If both tubes are affected, this is called hydrosalpinges. The tube usually appears distended, which means it is swollen with fluid.

Most often, hydrosalpinx is caused by a long-term infection of the fallopian tubes. This infection may occur due to a sexually transmitted disease or a ruptured appendix. Hydrosalpinx may also be caused if adhesions (scar tissue) or endometrial deposits (from endometriosis) irritate the fallopian tubes.

> With hydrosalpinx, infertility is often the first and only symptom that something is wrong.

Most women don't have any symptoms and are diagnosed only after they try to unsuccessfully have children.

However, some women will experience pelvic pain in addition to infertility, as it was in my case. Rarely, there may be some unusual vaginal discharge. They may also have symptoms of the root cause of hydrosalpinx. An example of this would be pelvic inflammatory disease (PID).

Blocked tubes are usually diagnosed during a fertility workup. An HSG—a special kind of x-ray—can show tubal blockages.

Surgery is the most common treatment for hydrosalpinx, with IVF treatment afterwards to aid in conception. Most often, the fallopian tube is removed completely.

Depending on the root cause of the hydrosalpinx, surgery may also involve removal of other adhesions, scar tissue, or endometrial growths on reproductive organs can lead to infections and an ectopic pregnancy if you do manage to conceive. These complications on the fallopian tubes have been provided for you to appreciate how a miracle could come out of one of the severest forms. It must be noted that there are other types of complications of fallopian tubes that have not been included in this book, which would otherwise exhaust the entire pages of the book.

Sources:

> Columbia University Medical Center: "Tubal Factor Infertility."
> Stanford Health Care: "Fallopian Tube Recanalization."
> Mayo Clinic: "Ectopic Pregnancy," "Tubal Ligation Reversal."
> Fairview.org: "Fallopian Tube Catheterization (Recanalization)."
> UpToDate: "Ectopic Pregnancy: Surgical Treatment."
> UW Health: "Fallopian Tube Procedures for Infertility."
> Medscape: "Salpingostomy and Salpingectomy," "Uterine Tube (Fallopian Tube) Anatomy."
> Hydrosalpinx: Fact Sheet. American Association of Reproductive Medicine.
> Conceiving After Tubal Surgery: Fact Sheet. American Association of Reproductive Medicine.

Kasius JC, Broekmans FJ. "Pregnancy Outcomes of Interventional Ultrasound Sclerotherapy With 98% Ethanol on Women With Hydrosalpinx." Am J Obstet Gynecol. 2015 Jan;212(1):118. doi: 10.1016/j.ajog.2014.09.018. Epub 2014 Sep 20.

How to Grow Your Faith in God for the Battle against "Fallopian Tube Blockage"

Thousands of books have been written on faith, hundreds of thousands of sermons and millions of words preached on this topic and yet for some people, it still needs nurturing.

> *Growing our faith is an ongoing project, one that never ends.*

We all have different battles we are engaged in. For some, it is the battle against fallopian tube blockage; for others, it's another major medical issue; yet for others, it is an issue with the liver or pancreas. Beyond the medical arena, others have battles such as marital, financial, or inability to maintain a permanent job, to name a few.

> *Although someone's battle may be "lighter" than yours or vice versa, all of us have our own battles.*

In an attempt to help you continue to have faith in God and his plans for your life, before I continue to tell you my miraculous story so that you can be in the best position to expect your miracle stories also mainly by faith, it is the ultimate dream of this book to inspire you to remain calm and pray in faith for that miracle you are expecting, particularly that thing that seems impossible to achieve. Faith in God is the key that makes all things possible.

Faith is like a seed, plant it in your heart and your mind. At the appointed time, God will give you a mega harvest of what you need just when you need it.

Colossians 2:7 in the New Living Translation says, "Let your roots grow down into him, and let your lives be built on him. Then your faith will grow strong in the truth you were taught, and you will overflow with thankfulness."

How do you grow strong in faith so you can overflow with revelation, blessings, and thankfulness?

It's a process.

Smith Wigglesworth, the anointed English Bible teacher and healer, once said, "How can one come to possess great faith? Now listen, here is the answer to that. First, the blade, then the ear, then the full corn in the ear. Faith must grow by soil, moisture, and exercise."

Feed your faith through the Word of God. Brother Kenneth Hagin said, "Faith begins where the will of God is known."

How do you know the will of God?

Read your Bible... Begin doing what it says and you will have a growth spurt in faith.

> *Psalm 34:8 says, "O taste and see that the Lord is good: blessed is the man that trust in him."*

The Message Bible translation of Psalm 34:8 says, "Open your mouth and taste, open your eyes and see—how good God is. Blessed are you who run to him."

Psalm 119:103 in the Message Bible says, "Your words are so choice, so tasty; I prefer them to the best home cooking. With your instruction, I understand life."

By feeding on the Word, you never have to wonder or worry about what to do next. The Word of God is alive. It is like food that nourishes our souls. Our faith activates the Word.

John 14:26 says, "But the Helper, the Holy Spirit, whom the Father will send in My name, He will teach you all things, and bring to your remembrance all the things that I said to you."

God has dealt to every person a measure of faith (Rom. 12:3 NKJV). But as a Christian full of faith, God doesn't want you to become stagnant. He wants you to *grow* in Him! Growing in Him means growing from faith to faith (Rom. 1:17 KJV). It means getting to know Him better and getting to know Him more this week than last week, and more today than yesterday.

> "So, then faith comes by hearing, and hearing by the word of God" (Rom. 10:17 NKJV).

If you want to grow in your faith, it starts by hearing, and that means feeding yourself with God's Word. When you hear God's Word, it changes you. It affects your worldview and alters the way you think. Is this talking about brainwashing? Yes—if brainwashing means washing your brain with the Word of God!

We want to see things the way God sees them, and we want to think the way He thinks. The good news is, there's an entire book filled with the way God thinks—the Bible. Open your Bible and begin to read. Get an audio recording of the Bible and listen to it as you go to sleep, as you get ready in the morning, or as you drive in your car. Get audio and video teaching from Bible teachers you can trust. We have hundreds of teachings and media resources available to you for free on our website in the "Watch" section. Additionally, you can subscribe to our podcast and listen to faith-filled teaching on the go. It's a great way to start your growth.

It's one thing to hear the Word…it's another to believe it. You may have heard for years that Jesus is Lord. You may have grown up in a Christian home and been taught that since you were old enough to understand what your parents were saying. But something happened the day you believed it. Everything changed. "The old passed away and everything became new."

Romans 10:9–10 says, *"That if thou shalt confess with thy mouth the Lord Jesus, and shalt believe in thine heart that God hath raised him from the dead, thou shalt be saved"* (KJV, emphasis added). You became a Christian from hearing—and believing—God's Word. That goes for every part of your Christian life.

> *When you read God's Word, don't hesitate to believe it.*

If God said it, it doesn't matter how you feel about it. If God said it, it doesn't matter what you've heard that's contrary to it. God's Word trumps everything else. You may be struggling with your health. You may feel sick. You may have gone to a church that says God doesn't heal today. What does God's Word say? It says:

"I am the Lord who heals you" (Exod. 15:26).

"By his wounds you are healed" (1 Pet. 2:24).

"[Jesus] healed all the sick among them" (Matt. 12:15).

If God's Word says it, the matter is settled. It's time to believe it.

Grow through Taking God's Word

"But I'm still sick!" you may say.

Once you've heard God's Word and made the decision to believe it, you need to make the decision to take it. Take hold of the truth and never let go.

Taking it means putting God's Word before your eyes and keeping it before your eyes. Every day, speak that truth. When you want to receive your healing, search through God's Word and find verse after verse after verse about how God wants to heal you. Highlight those verses. Print them out. Tape them on your mirror. Add them as the home screen on your smartphone. Speak them every day.

When you take God's Word, the world may be playing tug of war with you, but you won't let go of that truth! Read it, believe it, take it, and never let go no matter what comes your way!

"Faith by itself, if it does not have works, is dead... Show me your faith without your works, and I will show you my faith by my works" (James 2:17–18 NKJV).

It's one thing to read, believe, and take hold of something. It's another to act as though you believe it.

When you know that you know God has healed you—because that's the loving God He is—it's time to act like it. Wake up in the morning and thank God for your healing. You may feel sick; you may feel like not moving a muscle. But don't let your feelings stop you from acting on God's Word. You may not be able to do much yet, because sometimes, it takes time to get the natural in line with the supernatural. If someone tells you, "You look sick," reply, "No, I'm doing great because by His stripes I am healed!"

As you act upon His Word, you're allowing it to grow in you, settle in you, become active and strong in your life.

Hearing. Believing. Taking. Acting. When you listen to the Lord, believe what He says, take Him at His Word, and act on it, you'll find yourself growing in your faith like never before. Then, God's Word will be working in your life in a way like nothing else can. It'll be working in a life full of *faith*!

CHAPTER 5

God Is Up to Something!

Many are the afflictions of the righteous, But the Lord delivers him out of them all.
—Psalm 34:19

It was a usual morning in June 2016, my husband kissed me on the forehead and assured me it was all going to be fine. We went on to have our usual morning session with God. We prayed for the success of the surgery to remove my fallopian tubes. And then we headed for Inova Alexandria Hospital to get the procedure done.

In Inova, while we spoke to the doctor, I asked her if I can save my eggs. She responded professionally that I could save them.

I was prepared for theater. I looked at Jermain's face for encouragement, but that didn't work. He didn't know what to make of all this. I wondered where Jermain's head "was at." He flowed carelessly along the corridors of Inova; he touched walls and prayed ceaselessly. He had tears in his eyes when I was wheeled past him to the theater. Softhearted man, this one. It seemed that I was stronger than him at this point, but I didn't care because I loved him with everything in me.

There is something about the theater that makes me think about heaven—the bright lights, clinic officials in white robe, the exceptionally clean environment, and the systematic way everyone goes about their duties reminds me of the vision of heaven as revealed to John by God in Revelations 21:

> And I saw a new heaven and a new earth: for the first heaven and the first earth were passed away; and there was no more sea.
>
> And I John saw the holy city, the new Jerusalem, coming down from God out of heaven, prepared as a bride adorned for her husband.
>
> And I heard a great voice from heaven saying, Behold, the tabernacle of God is with men, and he will dwell with them, and they shall be his people, and God himself shall be with them, and be their God.
>
> And God shall wipe away all tears from their eyes; and there shall be no more death, neither sorrow, nor crying, neither shall there be any more pain: for the former things are passed away.
>
> And he that sat upon the throne said, Behold, I make all things new. And he said

unto me, Write: for these words are true and faithful.

And he said unto me, It is done. I am the Alpha and Omega, the beginning and the end. I will give unto him that is thirst of the fountain of the water of life freely.

He that overcometh shall inherit all things; and I will be his God, and he shall be my son.

But the fearful, and unbelieving, and the abominable, and murderers, and whoremongers, and sorcerers, idolaters, and all liars, shall have their part in the lake which burneth with fire and brimstone: which is the second death.

And there came unto me one of the seven angels which had the seven vials full of the seven last plagues, and talked with me, saying, Come hither, I will shew thee the bride, the Lamb's wife.

And he carried me away in the spirit to a great and high mountain, and shewed me that great city, the holy Jerusalem, descending out of heaven from God,

Having the glory of God: and her light was like unto a stone most precious, even like a jasper stone, clear as crystal;

And had a wall great and high, and had twelve gates, and at the gates twelve angels, and names written thereon, which are the names of the twelve tribes of the children of Israel:

On the east three gates; on the north three gates; on the south three gates; and on the west three gates.

And the wall of the city had twelve foundations, and in them the names of the twelve apostles of the Lamb.

And he that talked with me had a golden reed to measure the city, and the gates thereof, and the wall thereof.

And the city lieth foursquare, and the length is as large as the breadth: and he measured the city with the reed, twelve thousand furlongs. The length and the breadth and height of it are equal.

And he measured the wall thereof, an hundred and forty and four cubits, according to the measure of a man, that is, of the angel.

And the building of the wall of it was of jasper: and the city was pure gold, like unto clear glass.

And the foundations of the wall of the city were garnished with all manner of precious stones. The first foundation was jasper; the second, sapphire; the third, a chalcedony; the fourth, an emerald;

The fifth, sardonyx; the sixth, sardius; the seventh, chrysolyte; the eighth, beryl; the ninth, a topaz; the tenth, a chrysoprasus; the eleventh, a jacinth; the twelfth, an amethyst.

And the twelve gates were twelve pearls: every several gate was of one pearl: and the street of the city was pure gold, as it were transparent glass.

And I saw no temple therein: for the Lord God Almighty and the Lamb are the temple of it.

And the city had no need of the sun, neither of the moon, to shine in it: for the glory of God did lighten it, and the Lamb is the light thereof.

And the nations of them which are saved shall walk in the light of it: and the kings of the earth do bring their glory and honour into it. (Rev. 21:1–24)

Faith Is a Key Factor!

Every situation we face in life reminds us of something regardless of our faith, strength, or weakness. The difference in the life of a believer and for that matter mine is that the tougher things get, the closer I move to God.

The stronger hope I build around him and the more I look for instances in the Bible about similar situations He the Lord has spoken to and caused miraculous changes to happen. When I'm waiting on the Lord, my focus is drawn on the beauty of the place he resides; no wonder each time I enter the theater, heaven comes to mind.

At the back of my subconscious mind, I knock on the heaven doors and say dear Jesus we have a situation. Sounds funny, but that is the kind of relationship I have with God. That is how far I have personalized God in my life.

Everything was set for the surgery. Humanly, after paying close to fifty thousand dollars, my expectations were high, even if my tubes were removed, I would have frozen my eggs with the hope of holding a child someday.

> *God has said He will bless me with a child, but I didn't know how, but I embraced every opportunity to hold a baby with so much love and expectations.*

Expectations to see how God manifests Himself in my life.

The surgery was partially successful if I'm allowed to say it that way. Partial because they were able to successfully retrieve five eggs from the right, but for an unknown reason, the dominion fertility on the left side closed out on them. It will open for them to get inside, but when they try taking out the eggs, it closes down on them. So, nothing could be retrieved from the left.

All attempts to retrieve another set of five eggs on the left side failed.

I asked my doctor if they could do something about the eggs, and he fixed his gaze on my eyes and said nothing could be done at this point, resting his butts on a seat as if to tell me he has done all he could do and was tired. But faith will later be proved that there was more to be done to save my eggs.

Something was not right in my spirit because anytime we prayed after the eggs were retrieved, I felt in my spirit that God informed us that we were handling this case the wrong way.

Each time we prayed, I saw a woman touching the eggs, meaning God is telling us that is not the way we have to go.

> *When you are in tune with the spirits, understanding the things of the spirits follows naturally after every revelation.*

You get to understand why certain things happen at certain times. And you have the privilege of understanding things of the spirit. Some of them may include the interpretation of dreams, others may be the interpretation of visions. Things of the spirits vary. Work toward yours and enjoy your journey with the Lord because God is a Spirit, and they that worship him must worship him in spirit and in truth (John 4:24).

False worshippers either worship something other than God or they may attempt to worship the true God but do it in ways that actually dishonor Him. But either way, sincerity is not the only criterion for measuring true worship. All true worshippers are sincere, but all sincere worshippers are not true. For example, there are devout and sincere worshipers from different religions and backgrounds but we believe there is only one true God who reveals Himself through His word and continues to reveal Himself today in many different ways.

There are also Christians who are sincere, but their worship is man-centered. Sometimes, it's patterned more after the entertainment world than after the Bible. It draws attention to the performers but not to the Lord. Or, on the other end of the Christian spectrum, some go through ancient liturgies week after week, but their hearts are not in submission to God. They mistakenly think that because they went through the rituals, they're good for another week. They're like the Jewish leaders of whom Jesus said (Matt. 15:8, citing Isaiah 29:13), "This people honors Me with their lips, but their heart is far away from Me." So, we need to be careful not to fall into the category of false worshipers.

> *We should worship the Father in spirit.*

To worship in spirit is to worship from the heart or from within. It's opposed to formal, ceremonial, external worship by those whose hearts are not right with God (Matt. 15:8). Thus, the most important factor in becoming a worshiper is to guard and cultivate your heart for God. John Calvin

(Calvin's Commentaries [Baker], p. 161) says that worship in the spirit is the inward faith of the heart, which produces prayer, purity of conscience, and self-denial, leading to obedience.

I believe that worship in spirit is, in part, emotional or felt. This is not to say that we should pump up our emotions with music or crowd fervor. Genuine emotions for God stem from focusing our minds on the truth of who He is and what He has done for us at the cross. But if your worship never touches your emotions, something is wrong. It's like my love for my wife. My relationship with her is not built on my feelings, but rather on my commitment to her. But when I think about all that she means to me, I feel love for her, and I ought to express that love in some outward manner that shows her that I love her.

After the surgery, every call we received from the hospital was to tell us one of the embryos didn't make it. Initially, I would cry each time those calls from the hospital came in.

We didn't lose hope, we kept praying each day and night hoping to hear a positive result from the hospital, but every morning, the hospital called to tell us about an egg that couldn't survive.

These are eggs we had spent $50,000 to retrieve and get it fertilized to enable the doctors to replant them in my womb.

We kept losing them one after the other. The Bible says in Psalm 34:19,

> *"Many are the afflictions of the righteous, But the Lord delivers him out them all."*

Sometimes we hear the voice of the Lord; we see God communicating with us, but we just want to solve our problems on our own not because we doubt God or because we've lost faith, but we want to do something whilst waiting. We don't want to look idle whilst waiting. Be patient. But waiting without doing anything is not patience.

Wherever you are, reading this book, I want to tell you that no matter what you are going through, holding on to the promises of God, hold on to His words; don't try helping God out no matter what comes your way, don't help God out because you want quick result. He has His own times and seasons. When the time is right, He the Lord will make it happen. He promises because He can fulfill it.

We were left with one egg, which was okay, so they were able to freeze it. We were scheduled for the sixteenth of June 2016 for the embryo transfer at 1:45 p.m. at the Dominion Fertility Clinic.

On that fateful day, we decided to go to the clinic early to avoid any delay. A phone call came through and it was the doctor. I remember his words graphically as he said, "Hey, Sabina," and I responded calmly. Then he continued, "I know we have an appointment," and I responded, "Yes, Doctor, we will be there before time." There was an awkward silence from the other end of the line. He finally broke the silence. "I'm sorry. The embryo didn't make it."

I broke down in tears, I cried out the pain and disappointment; my husband held me close to comfort me. I was engulfed in so much pain, but I was not stripped off my faith. I knew God was not in favor of this procedure, but why did He watch on till I had lost all the eggs?

Like an emerging storm destroying everything in its way, I threw out all the items we have gathered for the doctor's appointment. As if everything in the room was the cause of my grievances, I was mad at them all, destroying everything that stood in my path.

> *I asked God why He had allowed it. The answer, I had no idea, was in the coming days.*

I felt a firm grip of assurance from behind. It was my husband... He was in tears too. I've always been his strength, but at that particular moment, I needed him like never before. The emotions that had filled the room crippled my joints and brought me to my knees. Tears were not flowing anymore. Right there at that moment, we held hands and thanked God. In my prayer, I said:

> The Bible informs us to give thanks to God in everything
> My duty and purpose on earth is to worship you
> I know I am nothing without you
> This morning all I can say is thank you
> This battle is not mine, Father

It all belongs to you; I am holding on to your
Word and your promises.
I want to come out victorious.

All this while, my husband had his hands tightly wrapped around me and kept whispering "Amen" amidst the tears.

As I prayed, a message dropped in my heart about the story of Job in the Bible. My Bible makes me understand that His ways were right in the sight of God. And God blessed him…

"In the land of Uz there lived a man whose name was Job. This man was blameless and upright; He feared God and shunned evil" (Job 1:1).

The devil told God Job love him because of his blessings, so if he wants to know the true faith of Job, he should take everything from him. So, he gave the devil the power to take everything from Job except his soul. Then Job started to lose everything he owed including his children, even in all his afflictions he never lost faith in God. So, when I think of this, I ask myself what at all will steer my faith from God.

Why Do Bad Things Happen to Good People?

An age-old question that many of us never cease to ask is:

> *Why do bad things happen to good people? This is one of those questions that people of faith have pondered for millennia.*

Why do seemingly good or innocent people suffer? Why do children die in natural disasters? Why are infants born with debilitating diseases and why do babies get cancer? Why do innocent children die even before they are formed, even when they are but embryos?

The first response is, "Who is really good?" After all, the Bible says that "all have sinned and fallen short of the glory of God." So, all of us are deserving of punishment and suffering. So really, bad things do not happen to good people because there are no truly good people.

The second answer is that bad things happen to good people because God chooses not to interfere. This is because many people have the idea that God is somehow detached from the universe. God started the machine going, and people have messed the universe up. As a result, bad things happen to good people because we have messed up the way the universe is supposed to work.

> *Our sin has thrown a monkey wrench into the internal workings of the cosmos and gummed up the machine.*

But that is not a Christian belief. God is involved in His universe. God does intervene in its workings to cause oceans to part and rain to fall or not fall and to heal diseases and save people. God even went as far as to come in the flesh in Jesus Christ. And Jesus didn't just teach, He also healed and then He died for the sins of the world.

So, I had to make up my mind that God was part of my world, He was present in my battle, and He was the commander in chief. He sat at the throne and presided over the affairs of this battle. That was where my hope came from—the mountains.

> *No matter how clever or resourceful you may be, sooner or later, we reach a point where we must reach out for help. We come to where we ask ourselves, "Where do I turn for help?"*

Some turn to the mysterious power of a positive attitude. The little red engine, "I think I can." "They said it couldn't be done…" A positive attitude is important, but it has its limitations; it is not omnipotent. You may be facing a solid brick wall.

There are those who would interpret this verse by saying, "Just look at how strong and majestic those mountains are," now say, "I am strong and majestic. I shall endure."

Some are always looking to friends for help. They seem to make a habit of it. Any little crisis and they cry; that's it, that's the last straw, and the phone they go. Then they wonder why they can't keep a friend. Being very practical, it is good to have friends you can call on. They too have their limitations. The psalmist said, "Help us, O Lord, for vain is the help of man."

"My help comes from Jehovah."

What does "looking" to the hills have to do with it?

Psalms of ascents as Jews made their pilgrimage to Jerusalem for annual feast days. So many would come through Jordan Valley. Looking toward the hills would be looking to Jerusalem where they were to worship Jehovah.

> "My help comes from Jehovah, the Maker of heaven and earth."

There is an irrational way of looking at nature. To look at nature and worship nature. The rational way is to appreciate its beauty and complexity and worship the God who created it.

The value of looking to God for help. His availability, "He that keepeth thee will not slumber." He is always there. One of the problems of learning is to rely on friends, who are not always there when you need them. His ability, "The Lord is thy keeper." So often we cry, "Help, Lord, I'm slipping." "He will not suffer their foot to be moved." "Lord, evil is about to overwhelm me!" He shall preserve thee from all evil. Now unto Him who is able.

At the end of our sorrowful day was the rising of a new hope, the certainty that our hope cometh from the Lord. Thus, we had no cause to panic nor fear for He is with us.

CHAPTER 6

The Challenges of Ectopic Pregnancy

Let us then approach God's throne of grace with confidence, so that we may receive mercy and find grace to help us in our time of need.
—Hebrews 4:16

I had one more tube to be operated on, but looking at the cost involved and what we have spent so far, we bet our coin on an Indian doctor who reviewed our case and had an interest. So, we secured our medical visa for the procedure and prepared for India. The battle between science and faith took us to the shadows of India where it seemed science had a comfortable lead. Up to the point where we had to travel to India, though we kept our faith in God alive, science was ruling us.

To reduce our period of stay in India from three months to about a month, the doctor suggested we get the first phase of the surgery done here in the United States. I thought it was a laudable idea. But as the hand of God would have it, the trip to India was canceled.

We went back to Inova Hospital to book for the prep surgery, but they didn't know which of my insurance card to use so I was asked to hold on until they figure it out.

Everything got sorted out, and we were booked on June 6, 2017, at the Virginia hospital for the prep surgery.

I can recall how we were physically drained from moving from one hospital to another. I thank God that He chose an understanding man for me as a husband, a man who didn't give up on me, not even once. Throughout all my appointments, he was with me. When all hope was lost, he kept pressing on, building my faith in prayer and in the words of the word of God.

The Joy of Having the Right Life Partner

In choosing our life partner, we need God's own intervention. We need men and women of God who are mature in the Lord, those that will stick by you when the path of life gets stormy. Not those that will be looking for a way out at the sight of any little wind.

I will want to agree on the statement that love is not enough for marriage. Be with someone who can complement your faith and growth both physically and spiritually. Someone you can totally trust and rely on because the journey and the struggle of life demands a bit of everything.

The Jawbreaking and Unexpected News!

The morning before the surgery, my husband woke up in the morning and said, "Sabina, I had an encounter with

God in a dream, and God told me you are pregnant. I heard everything loud and clear and I believe it."

This was not the first time God had spoken to my husband, we have experienced the voice of the Lord so many times and whatever he said He will do, He did it, most times, to our amazement.

I was at a point in my faith where doubting was not a close relative. I have programmed my heart, my life, and all that I am to the will of God. I am into Him so much that if He doesn't tell me the next step to take concerning any decision I become still.

> *Waiting on the Lord and His direction has brought me this far, so there was no reason to doubt the revelation my husband had in the dream.*

I was full of hope as always. We went to get a pregnancy test. We did the simple urine test, and it came out negative. I didn't doubt my husband, but he was so certain of what he saw and head in the dream that he didn't accept the negative results. I recall him saying, "Look, baby, God says you are carrying a baby boy."

I loved my husband for so many reasons, and his constant quest to make sure I was feeling okay at any moment in time is one of the many reasons I love him. We were like one person in two different bodies. We feel each other's pain and emotions at any given time. He felt my emptiness when the result read negative and wanted to assure me beyond every reasonable doubt that what he heard was not just an empty promise. *Science had again proved my pregnancy negative, but faith said the opposite of it.*

He always goes out of his way to ensure my comfort and sanity. I bless God for such a partner. I didn't doubt him, but maybe my gesture and the results of the various hospital reports scribbled on my face was not convincing enough.

I said, "Okay, baby, I believe you, but we still have to go for our appointment."

> *At the hospital, I told the doctors without much conviction that God had told my husband that I was pregnant.*

My doctor stared at me for a couple of seconds and said, "Mrs. Patterson, you know you cannot get pregnant because of your condition."

I felt the care and concern in his eyes, but it was not more than the faith I felt within.

I brought my Jesus game on and argued, "Doctor, I don't know why it's difficult for medical officers to accept reports of the spirits, but God has said it and I believe it. I'm pregnant."

He gave me all the possible medical reports to support his point that I can't get pregnant, and I was not going to give up on my God so easily. I also gave him all the reasons why those results were not enough for God.

I gave him instances in the Bible where Jesus made a way when there seemed to be no way. I said, "Doctor, in Luke 8:43–48…"

> And a woman having an issue of blood twelve years, which had spent all her living upon physicians, neither could be healed of any, Came behind him, and touched the border of his garment: and immediately her issue of blood stanched.
>
> And Jesus said, who touched me? When all denied, Peter and they that were with him said, Master, the multitude throng thee and press thee, and says thou, who touched me? And Jesus said, somebody hath touched me: for I perceive that virtue is gone out of me.
>
> And when the woman saw that she was not hid, she came trembling, and falling down before him, she declared unto him before all the people for what because she had touched him, and how she was healed immediately.
>
> And he said unto her, Daughter, be of good comfort: thy faith hath made thee whole; go in peace.

I made the doctor understand that my situation is not yet twelve years. I have held onto the cloth of Jesus awaiting

His miracle. It's just a matter of time for Jesus to turn and heal my disease.

We argued over it for a while, and he was as professional as he could be in order not to break any professional ethics. He said with a firm voice, "Should we then cancel the surgery?"

"No," was my answer. "I will go ahead with the surgery, but you can have it done on the right because God said the baby is on the left," I told the doctors.

He looked at me in awe and shook his head as if to tell me, *You need more of a psychiatrist at this moment.*

> *Most often, in our daily submissions, we leave God out.*

For the promises that has not yet manifested, we are to walk in it and proclaim it.

That day, in the Bible, when Thomas was waiting to touch the wounds of Christ before believing, Jesus appeared and said, "Blessed is Him that has not seen and yet believes." The Bible says in John 20:29, "Then Jesus said, 'Because you have seen me, you have believed; blessed are those who have not seen and yet believed.'"

On the fateful day of the surgery, the doctor questioned my certainty on the position of the baby, and I responded, "I know because God said it."

Doubt was written all over his face and he asked, "Do you want to cancel the surgery?"

To which I answered, "No, Doctor, I'm only telling you can go ahead with the surgery, take the ovary and eggs from the right side but not the left because that is where the baby is going to be." I was firm and specific. I knew God was up to something!

This doctor must have been in a debate club while in school. I felt we were staging a debate on faith and science. Or maybe he missed his Sunday school classes because he had more than a 100 percent faith in science but not a drop of faith in God, the Creator of heaven and earth.

If there should ever come a day in your life where you seem to have lost touch with God, a day when you will be engulfed in the facts and figures of the world just like this doctor, remember the Bible is not a book of fiction, neither is it a compilation of the thoughts of mortal men. If you can't remember any verse in it, remember the brief introduction to the Bible:

> *The Bible contains the mind of God, the state of man, the way of salvation, the doom of sinners, and the happiness of believers.*

Its doctrines are holy, its precepts are binding, its histories are true, and its decisions are immutable.

Read it to be wise, believe it to be safe, and practice it to be holy. It contains light to direct you, food to support you, and comfort to cheer you.

It is the traveler's map, the pilgrim's staff, the pilot's compass, the soldier's sword and the Christian's charter. Here too, Heaven is opened, and the gates of Hell disclosed.

Christ is its grand subject, our good its design, and the glory of God its end. It should fill the memory, rule the heart and guide the feet. Read it slowly, frequently and prayerfully. It is a mine of wealth, a paradise of glory, and a river of pleasure.

It is given to you in life, will be opened at the judgment, and be remembered forever. It involves the highest responsibility, rewards the greatest labor, and will condemn all who trifle with its sacred contents (From the Gideon's International Bible).

> *Put your faith to work and everything will work in your favor.*

We went about the debate for a while. The doctor would have canceled the surgery if he had his own way, from where I was seated, you could see the frustration and desperation written all over his face.

He was eager to change my mind on my decision. He said, "Look, Sabina, you don't even have quality eggs to get pregnant. Let's just get this done with." I just let off a mischievous smile that made the doctor fed up. He requested a pregnancy test to be run on me. I can never forget that date—June 5, 2017. I went ahead with the test with a full armor of faith believing I was pregnant, and the test came out positive!

I was pregnant. I praised the Lord! My doubting Thomas of a doctor had no choice but to cancel the surgery. For all this period of waiting, the one thing that has become common in my household was praying amidst tears. Tears became an uninvited guest that emerges whenever there was any announcement. I recall how we praised the name of the Lord in tears; the hospital staff watched on as we praised the Lord. I know the God I serve wouldn't put me to shame.

Our surgery appointment had to be canceled. We left the hospital full of joy and praise. I was asked by my doctors to have some rest, and I will be contacted for any further reviews and test to know how old the pregnancy is and to check the position of the baby in the womb.

Whose Report Do You Believe?

June 9, 2017, was a bright Saturday morning but not so bright with my health; I woke up feeling pains in my stomach. The pain got quite intense. I could feel my various joints go weak, so we had to go back to Virginia Hospital.

Upon arrival, a couple of tests were carried out on me, and it was then we got to know the pregnancy was a false one.

I was told the pregnancy is not a normal pregnancy; it is a false pregnancy, and surgery was required.

This report was delivered by a team of ten doctors. All ten doctors walked up to the side of the bed I laid as if the crowd was to emphasize the results.

I laid calmly on my hospital bed awaiting my results only to receive this report?

> *I asked myself, "Sabina, whose report are you going to receive? God has said it that you are pregnant, don't you believe it?"*

With that said, in my mind, I screamed, "No, Doctor." They had their usual mask of confusion on their faces and asked me why I said no. My response was quite straightforward and simple, "Because God said I'm pregnant, and the baby is going to be in my left tube."

I asked my husband if we could pray because something was not right. The doctors excused us, and I held my husband's hands in prayer.

That moment in the hospital room, we looked up to the heavens and sang:

> I will lift up my eyes unto the hills
> From where cometh my help?
> My help cometh from the Lord
> He said He will not suffer thy foot
> Thy foot to be moved
> The Lord that keepeth thee
> He will not slumber nor sleep
> For the Lord is thy keeper
> The Lord is thy shed

Upon thy right hand
Upon thy right hand
No sun shall smite thee by day
Nor moon by night
He shall preserve my soul
Even for forever more
My help my help
All of help cometh from the Lord.

And indeed, at that moment, I needed all the help the heavens could provide. For ten minutes, we cried unto the Lord in prayer.

> *In my submission, I told the Lord that it's His report I'm believing.*

Jesus is the Lord of my life. I have no other God beside Him. I'm trusting Him this very moment for a miracle.

I don't know what you might be going through this very moment, dear reader, but we are writing this book to let you know that the God you have trusted with your pain, your diseases, your debts, your life, or whatever it may be that is weighing you down is a prayer answering God and whatever He has said, whatever He has promised in your life, He will do it. Don't give up just yet.

The Jesus we are following went through a lot more than we are going through now.

No one has spat on your face yet, no one whipped you till you see blood oozing out of your flesh, and you have not been nailed on the cross yet.

Our Jesus faced all these and more not in spirit but in flesh and blood like you are now. He could have given up on us because we didn't deserve it, but He held on to the very end.

And as followers of Christ Jesus, we are not free from afflictions of the world. Psalm 34:19 say, "Many are the afflictions of the righteous but the Lord delivereth him from them all."

God didn't promise a trouble-free walk with Him, but the good news is, He said He will deliver you from all troubles and give you rest. Your duty is to hold on steadily onto Him.

> *Don't be moved or shaken by any wind that blows for in His time, He will manifest his glory.*

The doctors came back after our prayers to prepare me for the surgery. I felt renewed after the time of prayer. In the theater room, while everyone else prepared for the surgery, I was battling which side to believe, whether faith or science. I called the person in charge of the surgery and reassured him I was pregnant. And to render my stance valid, I had to prove stubborn by objecting to the surgery.

The doctor said they have done the sonogram, and I didn't even have a hip bone in my left to help carry a baby.

He insisted that my case was too risky for us to be going back and forth on it.

At this point, you could tell how depressed my doctors looked, and it didn't look like I was about to change my mind anytime soon, so I was admitted there till Sunday, June 10, 2017. That was the day I was asked to go home.

On June 11, 2017, I was directed to my obstetrician-gynecologist at Caesar Hospital; they also did a further test and still couldn't see any sign of pregnancy. We were not done yet; we were sent to Tysons Corner Medical Center for more information about my said pregnancy.

They also had a look at it and said it was a false pregnancy.

There at Caesar hospital, the doctor recommended a drug to kill whatever it is that was growing inside me because it was a false pregnancy.

The doctor was preparing methotrexate injection, an injection used in medical abortion to offer women early pregnancy abortion option that doesn't involve a surgery.

Methotrexate is also used for the treatment of ectopic pregnancy.

> *At that very instant, my husband had a Bible in his hand and the Bible started opening. And it stopped at a quotation. "Fear not, for I am with thee: be not dismayed; for I am thy God: I will strengthen thee; yea, I will uphold thee with the right hand of my righteousness" (Isa. 41:10).*

My husband then said, "Doctor, can I come in for a moment?"

The doctor then asked if there was any problem. He said not really, but the quotation being shown to me right now says fear not for I am with you. It means God is with us right now.

At every stage of our struggle, we felt abused constantly by the people who were supposed to be our caregivers. They constantly abused our faith, abused our religion, and this went further to stain our integrity. Some health personnel took advantage of our situation to even abuse us verbally simply because we were not in line with them.

The doctor then said to my dear husband, "Don't be stupid. This is how Christians end up dying all the time, you keep saying God, God, God. Your wife is battling with life and death, and you're sitting here telling me God says fear not, He is with you guys? There is no pregnancy. I want you to get it."

The doctor went on further to say, "That's how a man was drowning, your God sent a boat. Your man didn't join the boat, they sent a life guard; your man said no, they sent another canoe; the man said no, and he drowned and died and went to heaven, and God told the man you are being stupid. It's the same thing you are doing. After your wife is gone, God is going to tell your wife and you that you are being stupid."

The doctor meant to say God sent help to rescue the man, but he didn't see God in all of that; he was waiting to see God Himself pull him out of the water.

The doctor felt the way we thought of God didn't make any sense in the medical field. There was no way a pregnancy could come out of my situation in the medical world.

What they didn't understand is that we were not they because of what they have to say or do, we only affirm the directions and the prophecies of God. They were mere vessels God was using to glorify Himself, but to me, I felt these particular vessels were not ready to be used just yet.

After the doctor's speech, I told my husband, "We have to get out of here." That was on June 11, 2017.

On June 12, 2017, that is the next day, we went to another hospital, and they also confirmed there was no pregnancy.

On June 13, 2017, we ended up in another hospital. They also confirmed there was no pregnancy.

I came home a bit devastated.

I came home and said, "God, I'm going to pray for three days after that I'm going back to the clinic to check. If there is still no pregnancy, I will let them go ahead with the surgery."

Hebrews 4:16 says,

> *"Let us then approach God's throne of grace with confidence, so that we may receive mercy and find grace to help us in our times of need."*

I didn't want to interfere with the plans of the Lord. I needed to hear his voice to know the next step to take.

Before His throne of grace, I laid naked in spirit for three days without food, seeking His face and intervention.

These Bible verses were a source of strength during those trial moments:

> A shrewd person sees danger and hides himself, but *the naive keep right on going and suffer for it*. (Prov. 22:3, emphasis mine)

> The devil said to Jesus, "If you are the Son of God, tell this rock to become bread." Jesus answered, "It is written in the Scriptures: 'A person does not live on bread alone.'" Then the devil took Jesus and showed him all the kingdoms of the world in an instant. The devil said to Jesus, "I will give you all these kingdoms and all their power and glory. It has all been given to me, and I can give it to anyone I wish. If you worship me, then it will all be yours." Jesus answered, "It is written in the Scriptures: 'You must worship the Lord your God and serve only him.'" Then the devil led Jesus to Jerusalem and put him on a high place of the Temple. He said to Jesus, "If you are the Son of God, jump down." It is written in the Scriptures: "He has put his angels in charge of you to watch over you." It is also written: "They will catch you in their hands so that you will not hit your foot on

a rock." Jesus answered, "But it also says in the Scriptures: 'Do not test the Lord your God.'" After the devil had tempted Jesus in every way, he left him to wait until a better time. Jesus returned to Galilee in the power of the Holy Spirit, and stories about him spread all through the area. (Luke 4:3–14)

And it is impossible to please God without faith. Anyone who wants to come to him must believe that God exists and that he rewards those who sincerely seek him. (Heb. 11:6)

Now faith is confidence in what we hope for and assurance about what we do not see. (Heb. 11:1)

For we live by faith, not by sight. (2 Cor. 5:7)

Let us then approach God's throne of grace with confidence, so that we may receive mercy and find grace to help us in our time of need. (Heb. 4:16)

Consider it pure joy, my brothers and sisters, whenever you face trials of many kinds, because you know that the testing of your faith produces perseverance. Let perseverance finish its work so that you may be mature and complete, not lacking anything. (James 1:2–3)

You will keep in perfect peace *those whose minds are steadfast*, because they trust in you. Trust in the LORD forever, for the LORD, the LORD himself, is the Rock eternal. (Isa. 26:3, emphasis mine)

The LORD is a shelter for the oppressed, a refuge in *times of trouble*. Those who know your name trust in you, for you, O LORD, do not abandon those who search for you. (Ps. 9:9–10, emphasis mine)

Trust in the Lord with all your heart, and do not lean on your own understanding. In all your ways acknowledge him, and he will make straight your paths. (Prov. 3:5–6)

The Bible has always been my closest friend. It speaks to my situation. It leads me to God and rekindles my faith in the Lord when temptations arise.

Around that same time, my OB-GYN called and said that my situation is getting worse because my hormones are getting high and yet there is no sign of a pregnancy.

I asked them to hold on and give me just three days. After three days, if there's no sign of pregnancy, I will be at the hospital for the surgery.

I went back after three days of waiting on the Lord, and they had another test done to see if I was pregnant. That was when they found out there was a baby growing in the middle part of my left fallopian tube.

When they found out, they said no. This is getting dangerous because the baby is growing in the fallopian tube. A two-month-old baby was rapidly growing in there.

We moved from one hospital to the other in the first four weeks of the pregnancy, and they could not see the baby. They only saw evidence of the baby in two months.

That is when I said, "Thank you, Jesus."

My doctor then said, "Congratulations, you are pregnant, but go to the ER and let them get rid of the baby as soon as possible."

My doctor then went on further to say an egg is growing inside my tube, and if it's not taken out quickly, the egg will burst, and I will die.

I received the good news and the bad news all at the same time. They called an ambulance to take me to the ER, and I excused myself for a word of prayer.

After the prayer, I took the steps from the ninth floor and ran away because if I told them God says I shouldn't do it, it wouldn't make sense to them.

My husband was with me then, so we decided to come home and figure out what was wrong because we know the prophecy we had; we know what God told us in dreams and in revelations. How then was this happening?

> *To us, it was obvious God was about to do something out of the ordinary because what we were going through was normal.*

Up until now, we know GOD wanted us to have faith and go through the process. Most of the time, people don't go through the process we often seek easier and shorter way out.

I told my OB-GYN that God said I'm all right. It didn't sit well with her. On June 14, 2017, I had a call from the Alexandria Hospital to report there. I was getting ready for the surgery when the TV in my room came on and it was JOYCE Meyer, and she said, "God said He has put his son inside you so do my prophets no harm."

"That was a timely message," I said.

Right after that, the program went on commercial. I told the doctor, "God has sent a message and that we shouldn't harm the baby."

She then said, "Who delivered that message from God?"

She just didn't believe me.

They put it on the medical record that the patient Sabina says God has sent someone to tell her not to terminate the pregnancy. They did not release me until the legal team came in before I was released. That was the time I had to go back to the Alexandria Hospital.

I stopped seeing all other doctors until the fifth month of the pregnancy.

All the countless doctors we've seen had the same opinion about my situation, so I decided to stay away from them to a period when terminating the pregnancy wouldn't be an option any more.

One morning, I saw *pro-life* people protesting outside. I went to them and asked for help. They asked what I wanted, and I told them about my situation. They said they would try and find me a doctor; they did get me the doctor.

I went to see the doctor and he said, "No, it's an ectopic pregnancy. It's not going to benefit me so I should go ahead and abort the baby."

I said no as usual. I have come this far by faith, and I'm not turning back. Not in my fifth month.

Later on, Caesar also called me and said, "You are almost five months. You are not going to make it. Let's get rid of this pregnancy for your own safety."

When I rejected, they also suggested to me that there was no way the baby will survive including me because the placenta has invaded my organs.

So, a nurse called Dian came and said, "Why are you always mentioning the name of God?" She said, "The reviews from the hospital had you saying God was going to come in. There are other clients who kept saying God was going to come through in the surgery, but God didn't come in and they died. So, what makes my case different?"

I told her she should wait and see the God that I serve.

I couldn't believe I was supposed to endure verbal abuse again after all the rejections I've had from the various hospitals. It was okay if you doubt what I'm telling you about my God, even Jesus himself faced rejection, but what I wasn't going to tolerate was to stand and watch people of little faith tarnish the name of my God.

It became a confrontation, and I rebuked her in the hospital and said,

> "I know the God that I serve. I'm not going to sit down here for you to put my God down because my God is a God of miracles."

I was told if I was not going to take the life of the baby, then they are not going to help me. It was not within their discretion and power to help me at that point.

During that same fifth month, I lost the fluid on the baby and asked God where I should go, and He said, "Go to…"

I prayed to God and asked, "God, where do you want me to go?"

And He said to me in a voice as mild and gentle as morning dew, "Go to John Hopkins Hospital in Baltimore."

A Miracle Called…Judah!

Once again, I came alive hearing from my God.

We went to Baltimore and the first phone call I made, the woman on the other end of the line said I cannot come in without a referral because of my case. A doctor has to refer me to the hospital.

There was no way any doctor was going to give me the referral.

I went back to what I know how to do best—that is praying. I prayed and told God they are asking for a referral. They said I cannot come to the hospital without a referral, so please God make a way.

The second phone call we made, we were booked without a referral.

On arrival, they also confirmed the placenta has invaded my organs, so they were going to keep me in the hospital until the seventh month. Then they will deliver the baby.

By that time, God had already given us the date so the seventh month, they said, "Confirmed what the Lord has said."

After all the sleepless nights, tears, endless fasting, and prayers, everything came together in His time.

So, the surgery was performed on November 17, 2017.

The doctors were in constant fear and panic. I kept assuring them they shouldn't panic because God will come through; I didn't make any sense to them then. I told them the God I serve is a God of faithfulness. When I encouraged them, sometimes they take it, sometimes they don't; being a Christian is one thing, but having faith is another.

In my case, being a Christian was not the answer, but my faith as a Christian, because everything that I was doing, I was moving by faith because the Bible says blessed are those that have not seen but yet they believe.

That is what I was moving by, but the human aspect wanted to see the manifestation of everything I was saying physically before they believe.

I tried my best to talk to them and explained it to them, but deep down, I could feel their lack of faith.

On the day of the surgery, my husband was not allowed in because it was going to be an eighteen-hour surgery. We had friends, family, and church members pray with him outside.

I made them know that God said instead of the eighteen hours, He will make it two hours, and I will walk the same day.

God made it happen.

The surgery lasted two hours; I didn't end up in ICU, and I walked the same day to go see Judah.

Seven men appeared to me as doctors by my bedside and said, "Wake up and let's go and see the baby." Three of the doctors were on the left, three on the right, and one was in front of me.

So, I rose up in my pain with all the tubes and walked without any assistance to go see Judah.

When I got to him, he raised his hand and I said, "Yes, indeed, we made it."

Judah stayed in the hospital for three months. I was discharged a week later. As Judah was there, God manifested himself through Judah. On the day Judah was discharged, he was supposed to go home with feeding tube and his oxygen tank, but Judah himself pulled them out.

We came home without the feeding tube or the oxygen. God did not stop his miracle; the miracle continued from the beginning of our marriage to the birth of Judah, our miracle baby.

CHAPTER 7

Weapons of Our Faith

Finally, my brethren, be strong in the Lord, and in the power of his might.

—Ephesians 6:10

So far, you should have read a lot and gathered a lot of inspiration to hold on to the promises of God. However, this chapter will solidify your faith the more. You need to read this one last testimony to renew your faith in God.

Most of the times, God, in His own wisdom, makes us go through situations that shakes the very foundation of our faith in Him, but I'm here to tell you He is up to something.

One day, the disciples asked Jesus a question, which can be found in John 9:1–3:

> As He went along, he saw a man blind from birth. His disciples asked him, "Rabbi, who sinned, this man or his parents, that he was born blind?"
>
> "Neither this man nor his parents sinned," said Jesus. "But this happened so

that the work of God might be displayed in his life." Amen.

Sometimes, I read this Bible verse over and over again, and all that comes to memory is my fatal accident during my childhood.

> *I have grown to understand that God had to find a way to take out my left hip bone to create enough room for the baby to grow.*

I could have asked for a surgery to replace my missing bone. I could have cursed God when I became paralyzed. There was absolutely no reason to give up on God after He allowed the building to collapse on me.

One thing never wavered, and one thing never changed. I never lost my faith. I never ceased to go on my knees in prayers. I never ceased trusting and believing God to be the Lord of my life. I never ceased to thank God in any situation that came my way.

There were times when the future looked bleak, but he came through. He came through not because of my righteousness or faithfulness. He did come through because He is God.

He used me to glorify himself. I don't want to think about what would have happened if I preceded before God and went ahead for the hip replacement surgery. I wouldn't have been privileged to write this book to encourage you to affirm that faith in God conquers all things, all mountains.

How long have you waited on God? Do you feel alone and dejected? It's a perfect position to go down on your knees in prayers. Don't give up, that is exactly how God planned it. He is about to use you to glorify himself.

In the book of Ezekiel 37, He asked, "Could these dry bones walk again?" Brethren, this book is written to tell you that before God asks, He already knows the answer. He has a solution to them all.

Every single thing you are going through is for a reason, don't act before hearing the voice of the Lord, allow him to work and do everything in his own time. Ecclesiastes 3:11 says He makes all things beautiful in His time.

Kerry Haynes preached one day to his congregation about faith.

"Got faith?" He began by asking them one after the other…got faith? Got faith?

Remember the old milk commercials with famous people wearing milk mustaches? The caption at the end simply said, "Got milk?" It was catchy. It grabbed your attention. So, I thought about that when it came to naming today's sermon, Kerry said. We're looking at the famous eleventh chapter of Hebrews, nicknamed the "Hall of Faith." It's a listing of great heroes of the faith through whom God accomplished much. Heroes like myself and my husband. Like you and all the faithful believers who fought different battles of the Lord.

The question becomes, "How can I have that kind of faith?" Sometimes, we really need faith, don't we? Life is tough. And sometimes, we need to know that God is real, that God is aware, and that God is gonna get me through this.

So, let's examine faith. The chapter never defined what it is; rather, in verse 1, it gives a two-fold description. I've listed several translations of verse 1 in the outline as follows:

What is faith? Faith is…

"Confidence in what we hope for and assurance about what we do not see." (NIV)

"The reality of what is hoped for, the proof of what is not seen." (HCSB)

"The substance of things hoped for, the evidence of things not seen." (NKJV)

And when you want to carry a really big Bible to impress all your friends, grab the Amplified Version. It adds words in parentheses or brackets to try to further explain the meaning of the phrase. Faith is…

"The assurance (title deed, confirmation) of things hoped for (divinely guaranteed), and the evidence of things not seen [the conviction of their reality—faith comprehends as fact what cannot be experienced by the physical senses]." (AMP)

So, if these give us a description of what faith is, then what can it do for us? Verse 2 tells us the "ancients" or our ancestors were famous at it. We're going to look at two ancestors in particular: Abraham and Sarah. They point us to some very useful purposes of faith.

> 1. Faith helps us to make sacrifices.

Abraham has been called the "Father of the Faith." Verses 9 and 10 talk of his sacrifice on behalf of God's plan: "By faith he made his home in the promised land like a stranger in a foreign country; he lived in tents...For he was looking forward to the city with foundations, whose architect and builder is God."

Genesis 12 records God's initial call to Abraham. Basically, God said to Abe, "I want you to uproot your immediate family, leaving everything you've ever known, and go to a place you've never been. Now don't worry about where it is. I'll tell you when you get there." Sounds like your first PCS move, right? It took a lot of faith for Abraham to trust God. And it also took a lot of sacrifice. Abraham lived like a transient, in tents, never really settling down, like a refugee from another country. Sure, God was going to do some great things, like give him the promised land along with a ton of offspring who would later become a new country called "Israel." But God hadn't done any of that yet!

Abraham was seventy-five years old when he set out on this crazy new adventure, all because God told him to. A tent wasn't the nicest way to live, especially for a guy who was extremely wealthy through God's blessing. Yet, because he kept his eyes on heaven, he was able to put up with tents for now.

We all know about sacrifice. Some of you sacrificed in junior ranks or menial jobs for years before you got to where you are today. Some of you are thinking: We're done with sacrificing. Our time has passed! We're ready to live a little now and let someone else do the sacrificing!

Yet the truth is, God continues to call us to sacrifice this side of eternity. Perhaps God will call you to sacrifice your reputation to befriend someone in dire need of a friend.

> *Perhaps God will cause you to sacrifice your desire to be right and ask that relative to forgive you.*

Maybe you are sacrificing your pride by trying to witness to a friend who brushes you off. Their eternal destiny is serious to you but evidently not to them. Perhaps your sacrifice is stepping out into the unknown, trying to follow God when you're not sure where God is leading. For me, I sacrificed a hip bone so God could place a miraculous baby safely in my womb. Emmanuel was hidden safely in my left tube.

Whatever the cost, it's worth it! Someday, you will have a heavenly home that will make you forget all the hardships this life has ever brought.

Someday, you will have that building that Abraham longed for. You'll trade in your tent for a building in heaven. And the Master will say, "Well done, good and faithful servant! You have been faithful with a few things; I will put you in charge of many things. Come and share your master's happiness!" (Matt. 25:21). Faith helps us to make sacrifices. Or He may reward you with a baby, with a house, with your heart desires.

2. Faith opens our eyes to God's activity.

We have a new character, Sarah, inducted into the Hall of Faith in verse 11, alongside her elderly husband in verse 12. Listen to these two verses:

> And by faith even Sarah, who was past childbearing age, was enabled to bear children because she considered him faithful who had made the promise. And so from this one man, and he as good as dead, came descendants as numerous as the stars in the sky and as countless as the sand on the seashore.

"As good as dead." Poor Abraham! At ninety-nine, one hundred years old, his reproductive capabilities were about shot. But apparently, God had different plans. These two seniors were headed to Babies-R-Us!

Now before you get the wrong idea, please note: Abraham and Sarah weren't the perfect couple. They had their moments of doubt. They had times where they tried to help God out with disastrous results. Yet, the Bible still includes them as pillars of faith. That should give you hope!

Somehow, amidst all the doubt and questioning and helping God with their own clever ideas, Abraham and Sarah had enough faith to "consider God faithful" to keep his word, even when his words seemed impossible! Sarah was ninety years old and her husband a hundred when their baby was born! No wonder they named him Isaac, which means "laughter." What a joke!

From a man "as good as dead" would come thousands and thousands of descendants. It truly was a miracle! It was a miracle akin to so many other miracles recorded in the Bible: when Elijah called down fire from heaven at Mount Carmel, and then brought rain on command to stop a drought; when the Virgin Mary gave birth to a Savior; when Jesus took a little boy's lunch and fed a stadium, complete with leftovers. With God, miracles abound!

What kind of miracle do you need? Faith can open up your eyes to God's activities all around you.

Sometimes, I'll tell a veteran who is at wit's end, "You are ripe for a miracle!" Need to see someone's heart soften toward God? Ask God to show them a miracle. Need another dose of life? Ask God for the miracle of abundant life you can enjoy right now, even in your present circumstances. Need enough cash to pay the bills? Tithe on faith and ask God to stretch the remaining until payday. Watch what God will do when you look through the prism of faith.

3. Faith makes God proud.

Verse 16 says, "Instead, they were longing for a better country—a heavenly one. Therefore, God is not ashamed to be called their God, for he has prepared a city for them."

The Bible has various words for believers to remind us this is not our home: we are called "strangers," "foreigners," "sojourners," or "transients," just passing through. One of our church members recently asked me, "Pastor, is it okay to long for heaven?" And I replied, "Sure, as long as you don't try to help God get you there prematurely." After today, I could add, "In fact, it even makes God proud!"

Yet, it doesn't mean we give up on this life. You've heard the old saying, "She's so heavenly minded..." No, there are plenty of Bible passages that urge us to be salt and light in this world while we're here, to be active witnesses of love as Jesus was when he walked the earth. Yet, we can long.

The book of Ecclesiastes says God has "set eternity in the human heart" (Eccles. 3:11). We know there is more than just this life. We long for the life ahead. And it makes God proud!

I met a man not long ago with cancer at too young of an age, in my opinion. Don't ask me what age is right; there probably is none. He was just told his cancer is inoperable. When I asked him about his faith, he shared that he is a believer, yet also has doubts. I told him that was typical of most if not all of us. And we talked about heaven. I urged him to read a book like *90 Minutes in Heaven*, one of my favorites on the subject. And to continue staying active in his church and with his family, as he prepares for his eventual crossover into eternity.

Max Lucado, in his book, *He Still Moves Stones*, says, "Do something that demonstrates faith. For faith with no effort is no faith at all. God will respond. He has never rejected a genuine gesture of faith. Never."

The Shield of Faith

As children of God, we are admonished to display utmost faith at all times. In his book, *Spiritual Militants*, Charles Boison reminds Christians that "faith still enjoys importance as a central factor of a Christian's life as so many virtues hover around it." He continues to say,

> *"Faith makes giants look like grasshoppers and unbelief makes grasshoppers look like Anakims. Unbelief looks at difficulty, faith looks at God."*

One of the heroes of faith who understood and displayed practicalities of faith was the apostle Paul. For a minister of the gospel who spent more time in prisons than his own home, faith would have been one of his least favorite verbiage, yet he displayed more faith than could be imagined. Due to his numerous incarcerations, Paul likened the Christian as a soldier in the Army of God; he or she should put on the whole armor, outfit akin to a secular soldier. This is what Paul says in Ephesians 6:

> Finally, my brethren, be strong in the Lord and in the power of His might. Put on the whole armor of God, that you may be able to stand against the wiles of the devil. For we do not wrestle against flesh and blood, but against principalities, against powers, against the rulers of the darkness of this age, against spiritual *hosts* of wickedness in the heavenly *places*. Therefore take up the whole armor of God, that you may be able to withstand in the evil day, and having done all, to stand.
>
> Stand therefore, having girded your waist with truth, having put on the breastplate of righteousness, and having shod

your feet with the preparation of the gospel of peace; above all, taking the shield of faith with which you will be able to quench all the fiery darts of the wicked one. And take the helmet of salvation, and the sword of the Spirit, which is the word of God; praying always with all prayer and supplication in the Spirit, being watchful to this end with all perseverance and supplication for all the saints. (Eph. 6:10–18, emphasis mine)

Let us look at verse 16: "Above all, taking the shield of faith with which, you will be able to quench all the fiery darts of the wicked one."

"In all circumstances take up the shield of faith, with which you can extinguish all the flaming darts of the evil one…"

> *As long as we remain on this earth, circumstances—good or bad—may befall us.*

The enemy is also always at work. Thus, Paul alerts us to "grab" the shield of faith that would enable us to ward off, stop, or quench any fiery darts, arrows, spiritual attacks, and all kinds of circumstances from hitting us. It was faith that enabled us to withstand all the doubts cast at us, the insinuations, and the bad reports that were targeted at us during our time of ordeal. Had it not been our faith and persistence in God, we could have easily given up and allowed the negative "recommendations" of some of the doctors and other healthcare professionals to overwhelm us. And some of those recommendations were contrary to what God had told us. When all else fails in your battle in life, do not abandon your faith in God. It is a weapon that helps us to triumph in circumstances that natural weapons may not succeed.

This book was born out of our faith and strength in the Lord. Knowing very well that followers of Christ would face various circumstances in the spiritual and physical aspect of life, Paul urged them and subsequent believers to be strong. Considering the rejection, ridicule, and pain that we went through, we could have easily given up. Yet we held our head and faith high in the Lord, and He never left us alone. It is our recommendation that you would not give up, but "be strong" in the Lord. He has not disappointed anyone yet, and you will not be the one to break His record.

The odds that confronted us could not have been overcome or defied had we not applied these principles in the Lord. We were faced with both physical (scientific) realities as well as spiritual challenges that sought to subdue our faith in God. But in the end, faith triumphed.

> *It is our prayer that in the midst of circumstances, your faith in God will see you through.*

Sharing Our Faith and the Gospel

The gospel is the good news of Christ. We have to spread the word of God and to share our testimonies with the world. We have to tell others what Christ has done for us. Our goal is to share our testimony to help strengthen your faith as you read about the goodness of God.

Benediction

Let us pray:

> Father, you are good. You give us a yearning for you and for heaven. Help us to keep the faith. Help us to believe even when we haven't seen answers to our prayers yet. Help us to sacrifice where we need to, because this is not our home. We want to watch for your promptings and actions so that we can follow as you lead. Help us to keep fighting whatever battles you have adequately equipped us to fight. Like Joshua, we pray that you may continue the light of day that we may overthrow our enemies and be victorious to the glory of thy holy name. We ask these in the name of our Savior, Jesus Christ, Amen.

Just as He made me carry a *forbidden* pregnancy and bore a son to break all the laws of science and humanity, so shall He come to you at the point of your need. Amen.

Thank you for reading our story. It is our sincere hope that your torch never dims. Keep shining because unwavering faith can defy all odds.

Sabina and Jermain pose after reception on their wedding day

Sabina and Jermain ascend the stairs towards their wedding reception

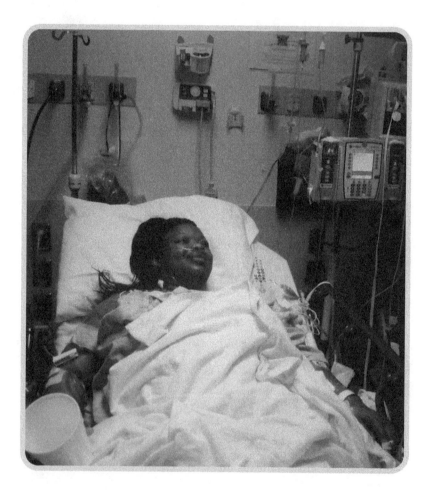

Sabina at the ICU recovering after the delivery of baby Judah

The trio—Sabina, Jermain, and baby Judah

Judah's first Christmas with mom and dad (Sabina and Jermain)

ABOUT THE AUTHORS

Sabina and Jermain Patterson have been married over six years and live with their three children—Jason, Jasmine, and Judah in Alexandria, Virginia, USA. They are a God-fearing family, who strive to praise and honor God in all that they do. The couple's unusual encounter, leading to their marriage and then to the miraculous birth of Judah Emmanuel, opened the flood gates for this unique and inspirational book to be published.

CPSIA information can be obtained
at www.ICGtesting.com
Printed in the USA
FSHW010607050521